Leadership—
The Inside Story

Leadership—
The Inside Story

*Time-Tested Prescriptions
for Those Who Seek to Lead*

Willie Pietersen

Rivertowns
BOOKS
IRVINGTON, NEW YORK

The epigraph is an excerpt from the poem "A Prayer Among Friends" by John Daniel, which appears in the book *Of Earth: New and Selected Poems,* published by Lost Horse Press. Reprinted by permission of the author.

Printed in the United States of America · September 2024 · I

Hardcover edition ISBN-13: 978-1-953943-40-8
Ebook edition ISBN-13: 978-1-953943-39-2

LCCN Imprint Name: Rivertowns Books
Library of Congress Control Number: 2024936343

Rivertowns Books are available from all bookshops, other stores that carry books, and online retailers. Visit our website at www.rivertownsbooks.com. Orders and other correspondence may be addressed to:

Rivertowns Books
240 Locust Lane
Irvington NY 10533
Email: info@rivertownsbooks.com

For William, Olivia, and Alexandra

Contents

Among other wonders of our lives, we are alive
with one another, we walk here
in the light of this unlikely world
that isn't ours for long.
May we spend generously
the time we are given.
May we enact our responsibilities
as thoroughly as we enjoy
our pleasures. May we see with clarity,
may we seek a vision
that serves all beings . . .

JOHN DANIEL

Introduction:
Our Learning Lab for
Leadership

Not only what we are born with, but also
what we acquire makes the individual.

GOETHE

A s a longtime president of various enterprises who has experienced the challenges of leadership from the inside, and now a professor at the Columbia Business School, I'm often asked to offer guidance on how to lead organizations. This is a fascinating and important topic—and it's also one that features conflicting theories of what works and what doesn't.

I believe that the world has taught us over the years that successful leadership is not simply a process of wielding power or making grand ad hoc decisions. Rather it is animated by set of personal principles that guide our actions and inspire others. Marcus Aurelius, the Roman emperor and philosopher, called this kind of internally driven, holistic philosophy our "command center."

Every effective leader I have observed has had a command center comprising their core beliefs, from international figures like Nelson Mandela, Ukrainian president Volodymyr Zelenskyy, and former prime minister of New Zealand Jacinda Ardern to CEOs such as Apple's Tim Cook and Verizon's Hans Vestberg, and historic role models like Helen Keller. They have been clear about the underlying values that have governed the way they lead.

We would love to have a ready-made recipe for leadership effectiveness. But it isn't that easy. Our challenges are contextual, and our approach must be suited for dealing with the specific problems confronting us. So we must build our own authentic philosophy. In the words of Candide from Voltaire's classic novel, *"Il faut cultiver notre Jardin"*—"We must cultivate our own garden."

Understanding this requirement, the best leaders are life-long learners, cultivating their personal gardens and drawing valuable lessons from each season's experience. They constantly learn from diverse stimuli, make sense of the shifting environment, and synthesize the emerging insights to develop their operating philosophy in tune with their own values and the challenges they face.

There's a wonderful Finnish proverb that says, "Everyone is the blacksmith of their own happiness." Ultimately, we are blacksmiths of our own leadership effectiveness, too. It's what we make of ourselves that counts.

In the chapters that follow, I describe a handful of evidence-based ideas that I think represent the main pillars of effectiveness for leaders at all levels. They'll illustrate the fact that leadership at its essence is an alchemy of compe-tence and character. At a minimum, leaders must possess the necessary expertise to do the job, but competence alone is not enough. Character is what builds trust in the leader and inspires others to be their best. It is the catalyst that converts competence into energy.

The sources of my thinking have been diverse, combining personal experience, reflection, observation, and study. My own learning laboratory has included five years of practicing law followed by 20 years as a CEO of several organizations. It now continues in my 26th year as a professor of the Practice of Management at Columbia Business School. I have also served on boards and as an advisor to numerous global organizations in both the commercial and nonprofit sectors. These experiences have enabled me to observe and learn from a wide range of leaders facing different challenges, as well as from the problems I personally tackled during my own years in the corner office.

The specific tools and practices leaders need to employ must evolve along with our changing world. I have strived to keep up to date with the latest research on leadership in the digital age. Managers today are seeing more frequent disruptions than ever before. Yet the underlying principles of success are enduring. They focus our attention not on what is new and often fleeting, but on what is permanent and important.

My views have been strongly influenced by two specific areas beyond the confines of the business world.

The first is the world of evolutionary science. The principles of this world, first articulated by Charles Darwin and continually refined and elaborated since then, tell us that the survival of any organism depends on its ability to adapt successfully to its changing environment. The evidence demonstrates that the same rule of survival applies to organizations—but with one important difference. In nature,

survival is a matter of blind chance, based on genetic muta-
tions that arise at random and affect the survival rates of the
organisms impacted by them. By contrast, organizations can
enhance their chances of survival through their ability to
learn intentionally about the changing features of the external environment and to adapt their behaviors accordingly.
Therefore, the most critical mission for leaders is to build
organizations that excel at this art of learning and adaptation. And that won't be possible unless those leaders become
continuous learners themselves.

I have also gained valuable insights about leadership
from my readings in two other favorite topics, philosophy
and astrophysics. I find that studying philosophy helps us
develop our personal answers to three life-guiding questions: *What is true? What is important?* And *What is right?*
And astrophysics brings us the humbling realization of our
own insignificance and impermanence in a vast, apparently
infinite universe that scientists now estimate to have existed
for over 13 billion years. At the same time, daily life continually reinforces the understanding that our limited lifespans
give us just enough space to make a mark.

In these pages, I've tried to offer "ideas with energy"—
concepts and guidelines that pass the test of being useful in
practice. They've provided the inspiration for my own philosophy and practice of leadership. I have not always lived
up to my own standards; as humans, we all fall short at

times. But the ideas in this book have served as my navigation system and basis for self-correction.

I hope they will also help you cultivate your own garden.

1. Building the Foundations: The Three Domains of Leadership

The price of leadership is responsibility.

WINSTON CHURCHILL

M y first informal tutorial in leadership occurred in the early stage of an eighteen-year stint with the Unilever Group, when I became the CEO of their foods subsidiary in South Africa. I was thirty-six years of age and one of the youngest people to hold such a senior position at the company—and I was acutely aware of how green I was. Unilever had placed a bet on my being an effective leader, and now I had to prove myself worthy of their trust.

I started with the mindset that running a business is largely an intellectual exercise, like a game of chess. I was preoccupied with concepts like competitive advantage, brand positioning, and business analysis. I felt that if the logic behind a decision was clear, people would recognize its correctness and do the right thing. Presto! The challenge of leadership, solved!

This was a view of leadership that was simplistic and incomplete.

Fortunately, I had a remarkable boss. C.J. van Jaarsveld, the chairman of the Unilever Group in South Africa, had a distinguished military record of fearlessly leading troops into combat during World War II. He was a natural leader—authentic and transparent, with an astute understanding of what made others tick. The ultimate straight shooter, he always told the unvarnished truth, but in a way that was somehow motivating because of his sincerity and goodwill. As a mentor, C.J. had a big influence on my personal development.

After three months in the job, I was called into C.J.'s office for a review. "Tell me," he asked, "what has surprised you most in your new role?"

I said I was amazed at how much time I needed to spend on "people issues" as opposed to operational matters—on challenges like making my team members feel understood and motivated and nurturing their personal development.

C.J. smiled and declared, "Pietersen, welcome to leadership."

Looking back on that conversation, I see that it marked the moment when I grasped the essential distinction between *management* and *leadership*. Management is about things; leadership is about people. Both are important. The challenge is to create the right balance between the two.

The Three Domains of Leadership

Fundamentally, leadership consists of three domains: Personal, Strategic, and Interpersonal. Our challenge is to become *integrated leaders* who are able to master and coordinate all three of these domains (Figure 1-1).

o *Personal Leadership* (Leading Self) is about cultivating deep self-knowledge, authenticity, and sound

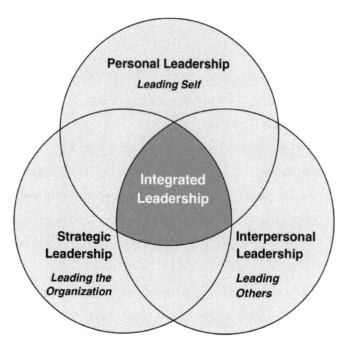

Figure 1.1. The Three Domains of Leadership

personal values. These are the foundations of character and the source of a leader's ability to persuade.

○ *Interpersonal Leadership* (Leading Others) is about understanding the needs of others, building strong teams and coalitions, and bringing out the best in everyone.

○ *Strategic Leadership* (Leading the Organization) is about setting forth a clear direction, a winning proposition and the right priorities for success, and then harnessing an effective method for achieving them.

General Edward Meyer, former U.S. Army Chief of Staff, said that leadership is like a diamond. A diamond is formed when three things come together: carbon, heat, and pressure. When any one of these is absent, there is no diamond. In the same way, the three domains of leadership are interdependent; when any one of them is missing or deficient, it undermines the effectiveness of the whole. Combining them successfully makes a fully integrated leader. Striving for excellence in all three is a lifelong learning process.

Stated in a different way, leadership involves running two interrelated systems that coexist in all organizations: a business system (Strategic Leadership) and a social system (Personal and Interpersonal Leadership). These two systems illustrate the interplay of competence and character that I mentioned in the introduction. Running the social system requires *character,* while managing the business system is a matter of *competence.*

Both attributes matter, but they are profoundly different. Character is expressed through a leader's individual values and the associated ability to inspire others. This is a strictly personal endeavor and operates from the inside out. Competence, on the other hand, involves the skills needed to drive an enterprise's operating effectiveness, and at its best it's a team effort.

As I lay out my ideas about leadership effectiveness in the following chapters, we will see how each of them relates to the domains of leadership named above and how they re-inforce each other. The three domains offer a unified way of understanding the critical components of leadership. What's more, the framework serves as a practical diagnostic tool that enables us to assess our progress on the lifelong journey to develop and constantly hone our individual leadership philosophy.

Above all, we should remember that the journey never ends. As Virginia Rometty, former CEO of IBM, likes to say, the key is to celebrate progress, not perfection.

2. Towering Example: How Nelson Mandela Achieved the Impossible

If you want to be a leader,
you must first be a human being.

CONFUCIUS

A gainst formidable odds, Nelson Mandela transformed racially torn South Africa into a peaceful, multiracial democracy. His example serves as an inspiring illustration not only of integrated leadership, but of a leader as learner.

First, let me set the scene. South Africa is a multiracial country with a population of about 60 million. Nonwhites make up 91 percent of the population, meaning that whites represent a small minority of just 9 percent. Despite this imbalance, white minority rule had existed in the country since the colonial era (from the 1650s until 1910). However, the apartheid regime, launched in 1948, took white domination to a radical new level of oppression and injustice. This odious system enforced rigid segregation between whites and non-whites in every sphere of life. (The word *apartheid* means "apartness" and, all too appropriately, is pronounced "apart-hate").

South Africa is also the country where I was born and raised. I witnessed the cruel effects of the apartheid system firsthand. Based on your race, you were told who you could marry, where you could live, where you could go to school, and where you could receive medical treatment. Interracial sexual relations were a criminal offense. Somewhat akin to the Jim Crow system that dominated the American South for generations, apartheid was an inhuman system of subjugation.

Today, it's widely recognized that race is, at best, a quasi-scientific concept with scant significance. But to maintain the apartheid system, it was necessary to treat race as a clear, unchanging set of characteristics that could be rigidly used to govern human relations. One especially odious piece of legislation gave a government board the power to classify a person's race according to a set of arbitrary visual and cultural criteria. The application of this law reached new depths when individual members of the same family were classified differently and forced to live apart, when courting couples were prevented from marrying, and when innocent children were forced out of the schools they'd been attending.

As a young lawyer, I had an experience that made these injustices jarringly real. I represented a number of young couples whose lives had been torn apart by this law and wished to appeal to the government board. The process required the aggrieved individuals to submit to a degrading personal inspection in which board members would examine them as if they were laboratory specimens—for example, inspecting the tint of a man's skin or twisting a pencil in a young woman's hair in order to measure its "kinkiness."

The first time I saw the impact of this behavior on individual human beings, my abstract concern about injustice was transformed into full-blown revulsion.

That night I spoke earnestly to my wife. We decided it was time to leave South Africa and make a new life elsewhere. As my exit route, I landed a job with the Unilever Group. In due course, I was posted to various overseas assignments, and eventually to the United States, where we settled down and became American citizens.

Mandela's Remarkable Achievement

From my new home in Connecticut, I followed events in South Africa with a keen interest. In reaction to the harsh apartheid laws, there arose a campaign of resistance with frequent violent episodes. The country seemed to be sliding towards a bloody civil war.

Out of this crucible, Nelson Mandela emerged as a leader of the resistance movement. Ultimately, he was apprehended, convicted of sabotage, and sent, along with other freedom fighters, to Robben Island, a barren outcrop off the coast near Cape Town, where he was to serve a sentence of life imprisonment.

Before the court handed down its sentence, Mandela foreshadowed the struggle to come by making this declaration while standing in the dock:

> I have cherished the ideal of a democratic and free society in which all persons will live together in harmony and with equal opportunities. It is an ideal which I hope to live

for and see realized. But, if needs be, it is an ideal for which I am prepared to die.

During Mandela's years in jail, pressure mounted on the white minority government from within South Africa as well as from the outside world. Eventually, the recalcitrant government leaders opened the door for negotiations that could lead to majority rule. In 1990, after 27 years in prison, Mandela was released, and as the head of the African National Congress—the leading party of the Black majority—he took over leadership of the negotiations with the government.

After years of wrenching discussions, the principles of majority rule and equal rights were finally accepted, and in 1994, Mandela became South Africa's first Black president. He now had the chance to realize his vision of a democratic and free nation.

But Mandela faced several major challenges. Nonwhite South Africans were bitter and hostile about the decades of oppression, and many wanted retribution. Meanwhile, the Afrikaners—the white descendants of mostly Dutch settlers who dominated South African society and government—resented their loss of privilege and were frightened about the prospect of violent reprisals by the newly empowered nonwhites. The nation felt like a powder keg.

Yet during his five years as president, Mandela achieved what many thought impossible. He led a peaceful transition from an adversarial, racially segregated country to a democracy based on the universal franchise, with a progressive constitution and an impressive bill of rights. In the process, he earned the deep affection and respect of all races in the country and ushered in a period of peace and stability.

Mandela died on December 5, 2013. In all the accolades he received from people across the globe, one message emerged clearly: *The world will be a better place if we can carry forward Mandela's values and not let them die with the man.* In that spirit, let's take stock by asking two key questions:

- How did Mandela help lead the peaceful South African transition from apartheid to multiracial democracy?
- What can other leaders learn from his life and work?

Underneath Mandela's monumental achievement lies a remarkable journey and a revealing portrait of a man's character. Let's examine his leadership effectiveness through the lens of the three domains of leadership I laid out in chapter one.

Mandela's Personal Leadership (Leadership of Self)

Mastery of self was probably the most remarkable aspect of Mandela's leadership. During his incarceration, he and his fellow prisoners were subjected to daily cruelty and humiliation, but Mandela conducted himself with courage, forbearance, and dignity. His moral fortitude was a beacon not only to his fellow prisoners but also to his jailors.

Mandela used his time in prison to think deeply about the personal and political challenges he faced and to muster his inner strength for coping with them. He studied widely, contemplated his future course if he were ever freed from prison, and clarified his vision for a democratic, multiracial South Africa. He steeped himself in the writings of Shakespeare, from which he derived profound insights into human psychology. His favorite passage came from Act II, Scene 2 of *Julius Caesar*: "Cowards die many times before their death; / The valiant never taste of death but once."

Pondering such sources of psychological and social insight, Mandela saw that the escalating anger and resentment within South African society would likely lead to a bloody civil war. He came to believe that his essential task was to save his country by finding a peaceful path to majority rule. What's more, his reflections led him to an essential truth: he first had to change himself before he could ask others to change themselves.

Of course, Mandela often felt anger over the way he and his fellow Africans had been abused by the white minority, and at times, he thirsted for revenge. But he also realized that giving free rein to these feelings would undermine his moral standing as a leader. So he trained himself to overcome his resentment and concentrated instead on building bridges of understanding across the chasm of hostility and fear. His lodestar was the maxim often attributed to Mohandas K. Gandhi, the fabled leader of India's independence movement: "Be the change you wish to see in the world."

Mandela's Interpersonal Leadership (Leadership of Others)

Along with this remarkable victory over himself, Mandela set about developing the elements needed for a successful campaign for unifying the nation, even while he was in prison. Most crucially, he trained himself to empathize with all South Africans, even those who viewed him as their enemy.

Consider these extraordinary actions:

- In prison, he learned Afrikaans, the language of his white oppressors, enabling him to converse with his jailers in their own language. He also studied

Afrikaner history so he could understand the origins of their attitudes.

o   He spoke respectfully to his jailers, took an interest
    in their daily concerns and family lives, and offered
    them advice where he could.

o   He even studied rugby, the Afrikaner national sport,
    and discussed the nuances of the game with his cap-
    tors.

As Mandela observed, "If you talk to a man in a language he understands, that goes to his head. If you talk to
him in *his* language, that goes to his heart." Over time,
through behaviors like these, he earned the profound respect and admiration of his jailers.

Later, after being freed, Mandela conducted his negotiations with the Afrikaner leaders in the same spirit. He drew
on his knowledge of Afrikaner history to acknowledge the
heroes of his adversaries, demonstrating to them that he understood who they were and what they cared most deeply
about. Acts of empathy like these made it possible for Mandela to be recognized and accepted as the leader of the entire
South African nation and to rally all its people behind his
vision of a better shared future.

When Mandela was inaugurated as president in 1994,
one of the guests and admirers sitting on the stage with him

was James Gregory, an Afrikaner who had been his chief jailer at Robben Island.

In 1995, the Third Rugby World Cup was staged in South Africa. Mandela defied the objections of the African National Congress by publicly supporting the predominantly Afrikaner Springbok team. This was a breathtaking decision and a bold risk. Up to then the nonwhites had regarded the South African team as a hated symbol of apartheid and always cheered for foreign teams during competitions.

The Springboks survived four grueling rounds of the World Cup and squared off against New Zealand in the final match. Regulation play ended with the score 9 to 9, forcing overtime. When the Springboks won it all with a decisive overtime goal, Mandela seized the moment. In front of a TV audience of millions, he donned a Springboks jersey and cap and personally presented the championship cup to South African captain François Pienaar.

It was a huge unifying moment for the nation. Tokyo Sexwale, previously a fellow prisoner with Mandela, observed, "That was the moment I understood that the struggle was not so much about liberating the blacks from bondage, it was about liberating white people from fear."

Perhaps most important, Mandela sponsored the establishment of a Truth and Reconciliation Commission that led the whole nation through a unique process of confronting its ugly past and undertaking the painful but uplifting journey of forgiveness and reunification. The commission invited victims of gross human rights violations under apartheid to give statements about their treatment. Perpetrators of these acts who gave honest testimony and showed remorse could receive immunity from prosecution. Those who refused or lied were put on trial and punished if found guilty. This collective stock-taking provided a healing process that allowed everyone to summon up their better selves. And in the end, they felt that *they* had brought about the reformation of South African society, which gave them a sense of collective ownership and largely defused the potential for festering resentment and hatred.

Mandela's interpersonal effectiveness stemmed from his extraordinary mastery of self, coupled with his profound empathy—the ability to see the world through the eyes of others.

Mandela's Strategic Leadership (Leadership of the Nation)

Management guru Peter Drucker said, "The first task of a leader is to be the trumpet that sounds a clear sound." Referring back to the third domain of leadership, did Mandela define a clear goal and priorities, and did he harness an effective method for reaching these?

Consider the speech Mandela gave on November 2, 1990, when he was released from prison. As a political leader in almost unprecedented circumstances, he had to walk a tightrope, offering a hand of friendship to the white community while assuring his Black compatriots that he would not forget their sufferings or ignore their grievances. His words made clear that he intended to represent all South Africans: "We must not allow fear to stand in our way. A united non-racial South Africa is the only way to peace and racial harmony."

True to his words, he achieved his goal of a peaceful transition to democracy and majority rule. On the political front, it is unarguable that Mandela's strategic leadership was stunning.

On the social and economic fronts, however, there have been shortcomings. After an initial period of growth in the new, democratically led South Africa, economic stagnation has ensued and in many cases the inequality gaps have widened. Furthermore, corruption has been a growing problem under his successors.

As we look at the scorecard, the first lesson is a simple reminder: no leader is perfect. In every case, we can point to failures as well as triumphs. It is clear that Mandela did not solve all the problems facing the country during his tenure. Does this mean Mandela was a failed leader? Far from it. Deeply embedded injustices are not vanquished all at once.

South Africa faces the same challenge Mandela himself faced, as defined in the title of his autobiography: *A Long Walk to Freedom*. The transition he led was momentous, but it marked the commencement of a journey, not its completion. It is now up to others to carry forward his values and continue that journey.

Compare his legacy with that of Abraham Lincoln, who saved the Union and freed the slaves—yet it took a hundred years for comprehensive civil rights legislation to be enacted in the United States, and racial inequality and injustice remain problems for the nation to this day. Like Lincoln, Mandela established the essential foundations of a great cause that transcended his lifetime, and in doing so created a stirring example of leadership for us all to learn from.

Mandela was inspired by his favorite poem, "Invictus," by William Ernest Henley. The title is Latin for "unconquered." Its final verse reads:

It matters not how strait the gate,
How charged with punishment the scroll,
I am the master of my fate,
I am the captain of my soul.

Nelson Mandela taught us that in order to bring about transformational change, specific leadership qualities are essential—namely, a combination of vision, principles, courage, and, most of all, the kind of profound empathy he displayed to promote reconciliation between mutually hostile factions of society. These attributes were built on the bedrock moral foundations of his character and his genuine affection for his fellow human beings.

As we consider other elements of leadership in the remaining chapters of this book, let's keep Mandela's moral and personal example in mind. Continual learning, farsighted strategic thinking, smart decision-making: all these are important tools in any leader's kit. But without a solid foundation in character, they won't yield the kinds of sustainable benefits for humankind that the true leader should always seek.

3. Learning to Learn: The Unrecognized Leadership Imperative

Truth is discovered, not taught.

MARCEL PROUST

A s Nelson Mandela demonstrated so well, a hallmark of effective leaders is that they are lifelong learners. Success is not bestowed on us; we must *learn* our way there.

In a 1997 article in the *Harvard Business Review* titled "The Living Company," Arie de Geus, then the head of planning at the Royal Dutch Shell Company, made a prescient declaration that has lingered in my memory: "In the future, the ability to learn faster than competitors may be the only sustainable competitive advantage." I suggest that this statement represents the basic formula for progress in any field of human endeavor—especially for leaders, whose duty is to light the way for others.

Although the challenges are greater in today's dynamic world, this is not just a modern phenomenon. Learning has been at the core of human progress over millennia, as our species discovered how to make tools, use fire, grow crops, and harness the powers of steam and electricity, ultimately ushering in the Internet and today's era of the knowledge economy.

At an early stage of this historic journey, two species of human beings—*Homo sapiens* and Neanderthals—coexisted and competed for survival in Europe for several thousand years (currently estimated to be between 40,000 and 46,000 years ago). Ancient bones discovered in caves suggest that Neanderthals were larger and stronger than our ancestors, and on average their brains were actually larger than those of modern humans. But while *Homo sapiens* survived, spread across the Earth, and flourished, the Neanderthals passed from the scene—with the partial exception of the scant remains of Neanderthal DNA, preserved through interbreeding and still found in one to four percent of modern humans.

Why did *Homo sapiens* win this battle for survival?

Anthropologists have long debated what caused the mysterious extinction of the Neanderthals as a separate species. Was it a plague? A famine? Were they slaughtered in an epic war? A persuasive theory is that it was none of the above. *Homo sapiens* probably won the contest because they were simply better learners, cooperated better with each other, and outmaneuvered the physically more powerful Neanderthals in the competition for the best means of survival. Deprived of access to vital resources, the Neanderthals perished.

The arc of human history provides a powerful affirmation of de Geus's dictum that effective learning is the key to adaptation, and indeed to ultimate survival. Today, this principle has become acutely true for organizations as they confront the rapid changes of the digital age. A crucial task for leaders in this disruptive environment is to teach their organizations to build resilience by becoming successful learning systems. But for this to happen, leaders must first become effective learners themselves.

The Wellsprings of Learning

How do we become successful learners? The challenge is that while we all learn intuitively, most of us don't really know consciously *how* we learn. As James Clear points out in his book *Atomic Habits*, "The process of behavior change always starts with awareness." The same idea is found in a well-known saying often attributed to Carl Jung: "Until you make the unconscious conscious, it will direct your life and you will call it fate." The point is that improvement in learning is possible only if we understand the internal drivers that propel us to success.

Margaret Wheatley, a well-known business consultant and complexity theorist, provides a compelling way to think about how we learn. She states, "You cannot change a living thing from the outside. You can only *disturb* it, so it changes itself." When I first read this observation years ago, it provoked something of an epiphany for me. It helped me realize that successful leadership is mainly about how we learn and grow in response to the disturbances and stimuli that life offers us.

Many of these disturbances come to us unbidden—naturally so, since most people don't like being disturbed. This is especially true of leaders, whose job is often viewed as centering on keeping their organizations' productive engines running smoothly and efficiently. Any outside force that disrupts the operation is considered unwelcome. But when we resist disturbances in this way, we miss the opportunity to learn from them and adapt successfully to changing realities. That's why the best leaders intentionally embrace outside stimuli as part of their lifelong quest for learning.

The disturbances that animate learning can come from many sources; meaningful experiences, the actions of teachers or role models, on-the-job challenges, disappointing failures, unanticipated successes, shifts and trends in the world around us, and much more. We can all think of the various influences in our lives, and how they have helped us learn and grow. Most of them first appeared in our lives as disturbances of one sort or another.

How I Honed My Knowledge of Finance

In chapter one, I wrote about my first experience as a CEO. Having risen through the marketing function, I knew very little about finance and was a little worried that this might show me up. This anxiety was the disturbance I needed to tackle a new learning task. I decided to come clean and confess the gap in my knowledge to my boss, C.J. van Jaarsveld.

"Okay," he said matter-of-factly, "Let's get you a quick education." C.J. arranged for me to spend a day with a financial specialist. But, candidly, this was a bust. The man took me through the arcane aspects of accounting and cited endless details without clarifying the underlying concepts.

The confusing recitation of numbers simply clouded my mind.

I didn't want to embarrass C.J. by telling him that his tutor had failed. But I needed to address the problem before too long. At a meeting soon after, a young accountant in my organization named Norman Peddie caught my eye. Norman sparkled with eagerness and regularly jumped into discussions to clarify complex issues. He had a talent for cutting to the core of a problem. I had found my teacher!

Norman was a few rungs below me in seniority and looked to me as an authority on running a business, but I buried my pride, called him into my office, and plunged in. "Norman, will you please teach me what I need to know about finance?"

At first, he thought I was joking. But when he saw I was serious, he realized he had an important job to do in educating his boss. We spent a series of two-hour sessions as Norman took me systematically through the key aspects of finance in a clear, simple way. He beamed with delight as his student absorbed the lessons. It was an enjoyable experience for us both. Although I didn't ask Norman to keep these tutorials a secret, he never breathed a word of them to others. Thereafter, when I reviewed the financial picture of the company at monthly staff meetings—and did so competently!—I noticed Norman quietly smiling with pride.

Through my subsequent years as a CEO and since then, I have continued to build on the foundations Norman taught me, systematically honing my knowledge of operating finance and thereby turning a weakness into a strength. Today, I regularly teach the subject to corporate executives at Columbia Business School. I particularly enjoy doing for others what Norman did for me.

This experience early in my leadership journey primed me to appreciate the value of being a lifelong learner.

Curiosity: The Avenue to Lifelong Learning

Shortly after I became an American citizen, my son and daughter finished high school. Where I was raised in South Africa, this event is exclusively called a *graduation*—a term that suggests the *end* of something. But in the United States, these milestones also have another name—a *commencement*, meaning the *beginning* of something. I like this term, because it exactly conveys the essence of learning as a way of life, not a one-and-done enterprise.

Oliver Wendell Holmes, the famous Supreme Court justice, serves as an inspiring example. When Holmes was 91 and in retirement, President Franklin D. Roosevelt paid him a visit and found him reading Plato. Roosevelt asked him why, to which the old man replied, "To improve my mind."

Learning is an active search. The dominant driver is curiosity. By this I don't mean idle curiosity that just prompts us to wonder why, but energetic curiosity that impels us to find answers—that seeks out disturbing stimuli and uses them as springboards for the discovery of fresh insights.

A 2020 BBC program that investigated the mainsprings of creativity generated some fascinating results. The researchers confirmed that, while each of us starts with a different level of creative talent, we all have the capacity to grow beyond that baseline. Their interviews showed that the main impetus for generating breakthrough thinking is the deliberate exposure, with an inquiring mind, to a wide variety of stimuli—different people, experiences, conversations, books, places.

Habits That Embed Learning

Learning is complete only when it changes behavior. To act on it, we must first be able retain what we have learned. However, insights are soon lost in the ferment of everyday life. So an important element in learning to learn is improving our ability to recall what we've learned and to embed it in our everyday behavior.

Hermann Ebbinghaus, a nineteenth-century psychologist, made a study of human memory. He was stunned to discover that our dominant trait is not our ability to remember—it is our capacity to *forget*. To illustrate this, he developed his famous "forgetting curve" (Figure 3-1).

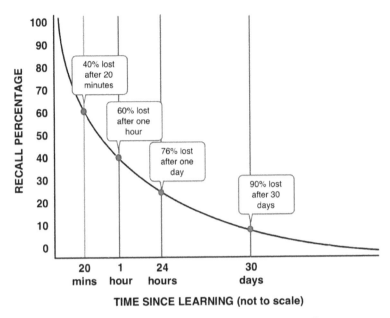

Figure 3.1. The Ebbinghaus Forgetting Curve

The findings are dramatic. In the absence of counter-measures, the average person loses up to 90 percent of new information after 30 days! For those of us who are determined to make good use of learning to improve our leadership capabilities, this is disheartening.

Fortunately, Ebbinghaus didn't stop there. He prescribed three antidotes to forgetting that build on each other:

o   Record new learning promptly

- ○ Review the lessons learned regularly
- ○ Apply the lessons in practice

The first habit lays the foundations for the other two. These recorded insights are what Ebbinghaus called "your savings." The second and third habits ensure that you derive a good return on those savings.

The Value of Keeping a Learning Journal

A powerful practice is to keep a learning journal to preserve your savings. I began this practice when I was sixteen. In an effort to expand my vocabulary, I started to write down the definitions of new words in a handy, easy-to-carry note-book. Gradually this process expanded into recording new information from diverse fields of knowledge such as philosophy, astrophysics, evolutionary theory, economics, and history. I now have a collection of learning journals, representing many years' worth of ideas and insights. I regularly review them during times of reflection and draw on them in my teaching and writing.

My friend Dr. Ash Tewari goes a step further. Ash was one of the pioneers of robotic surgery and is now the chairman of urology at the Icahn School of Medicine at Mount Sinai Hospital in New York. As the leader of his organization's surgical team, he strives to attract the best people in the field—researchers, sub-specialists, surgical residents, support staff, and so on. His driving passions are making scientific breakthroughs that benefit his patients and improving the knowledge and skills of everyone in his team. He is a rare combination of scientist, practitioner, and inspirational leader.

Ash receives hundreds of applications from ambitious and brilliant young people who are eager to join his team. But he has one non-negotiable requirement: to make the cut as members of his group, they must each keep a learning journal, something he himself does religiously. Ash's "savings" are beautifully handwritten and often illustrated with drawings. His journals have leather covers to emphasize their value. His practice is not just to write down his insights; above them, he notes the question being addressed. As a master of learning, he understands something important: defining and recording the pertinent question helps to clarify and deepen the answer. He stresses, "To write is to think."

Ash takes steps to help his team members deliberately carve out the time to reflect. At his weekly meetings, before they review their current case load, Ash sets aside time for the team to learn by calling on members (including himself) to share and discuss the insights they've recorded in their journals.

Ash has created a team of continuous learners and pioneers of best practices. He understands that learning happens only if we instill the habits that make it happen.

As we each consider how to pursue our own avenues of growth, we come back to Margaret Wheatley's insight. Our development as leaders, she reminds us, must be self-generated. Our task is to search widely for the stimuli that will light the way to learning and growth. In subsequent chapters, we'll explore not only formal practices such as learning-based strategies, but also the mind-opening pleasures of walking and the rich insights about life I derived from my cross-species relationship with my black Lab, Maisie. Almost everything in the world around us can be a source of learning if we approach it in the spirit of curiosity and exploration—an essential practice for anyone seeking to develop their personal command center for leadership.

4. Barriers to Truth: Discovering and Overcoming Our Hidden Biases

We don't see the world as it is, we see it as we are.

ANAÏS NIN

One of the biggest challenges facing leaders in today's dynamic environment is to make sense of complexity. This requires a competency that is crucial but rare: *critical thinking*. As the historian Will Durant observed, "Most people think with their hopes or fears or wishes rather than with their minds." The truth is that none of us is totally objective. Human beings are not wired that way. We are all subject to various biases that can distort our thinking and impair our ability to adapt to changing circumstances. Ironically, one pervasive bias is our tendency to believe that everyone else is biased except us! And since all of us are prone to biases that make our thinking unreliable, the same applies to the organizations we run—just on a larger scale.

Addressing reality is tough work. Developmental psychologist Howard Gardner calls our biases "engravings on the brain" that require "mental bulldozers" to clear them out of the way. To be effective learners, it is essential that we develop an explicit awareness of these barriers to truth. This ability to monitor our own thinking will arm us with the mental bulldozers to overcome our ingrained biases.

An excellent book on this topic is *Thinking, Fast and Slow* by Daniel Kahneman. Kahneman provides a comprehensive survey of the various biases that can trip us up. Below I examine four of the most problematic biases I have observed in my consulting work as executives wrestle with generating truth-based insights to guide their decisions: *the confirmation bias, the status quo bias, denial,* and *siloed thinking.*

The Confirmation Bias

This is probably the most prominent of all our biases. It is the tendency we all share to approach an issue with a pre-conceived idea of what's true, then seize on evidence that confirms what we already believe and disregard all contradictory evidence.

The confirmation bias arises because our minds are almost never a blank slate; we come to any new question with a prior view on how the world works and with an ingrained tendency to align our thinking about the new issue with the beliefs we already have. Thus, we tend to argue backwards from our existing beliefs, using selective reasoning to produce a plausible rationalization rather than an objective view of reality. It is extraordinarily hard to suspend judgment and analyze any problem with a totally open mind— the hallmark of critical thinking.

There are countless examples of people and organizations that have made badly flawed decisions under the influence of the confirmation bias. Consider the tragic collapse of General Motors (GM) into insolvency before it was rescued by the U.S. government. In the 1980s, GM controlled over 50 percent of the North American auto market and seemed unassailable. Complacency set in, and product quality slipped. Toyota and Honda seized the opportunity with superior quality cars at reasonable prices. GM's volume went into a steep decline, and its profits plunged.

Confronted with this serious challenge, GM's leaders had to diagnose the problem accurately if they hoped to solve it. Unfortunately, there was a preconceived explanation that GM was all too ready to embrace. Having run up costs over the years, GM's executives automatically blamed their competitive dilemma on a "cost disadvantage" relative to other manufacturers, taking this belief as an unquestioned article of faith. Believing what it wanted to believe, GM responded to the crisis by instituting a relentless series of cost cuts, even as its sales volume continued to decline. Of course, the cost cuts did nothing to remedy the quality problems that customers perceived with GM's cars. Buyers continued to desert GM's brands, and the firm's market share dropped to under 20 percent before it went broke.

What brought GM down was falling prey to their entrenched confirmation bias. Their demise was not caused by a cost problem but by a value problem. Their strategy was the equivalent of a patient suffering from liver disease but being treated for kidney failure instead. Fixated on cost cutting, the company's leaders ignored the quality deficit—the root cause of their market share collapse—until it was too late.

The Status Quo Bias

When confronted by the upheavals of a changing environment, we have a natural tendency to cling to the world we know. This is where we find safety and a sense of control. For as long as possible, we go on repeating the comforting mantra, "If it ain't broke, don't fix it." This is the status quo bias, a mental state that locks us into yesterday's logic.

In my seminars, I often ask executives what percentage of their financial results in the prior year was caused by decisions they made in that year. After some cogitation, they offer me their best estimates, with the average answer hovering at about 30 percent. This tells us something important: often, the largest part of an organization's present results comes simply from "surfing" on past momentum. This easily lures us into the illusion that we are generating ongoing success. Yet without fresh initiatives to meet the changing competitive demands, these results will soon fizzle.

Ironically, it turns out that one of the biggest causes of failure is the way we deal with success. The words to live by should be, "If we don't fix it, it will break."

Think of Kodak, once an American icon. At its height, the company commanded 90 percent of photographic film sales and 85 percent of camera sales in the United States. In 1996, Kodak was the fifth most valuable brand in the world. But despite this dominance, it was decimated by its failure to adapt to the digital photography revolution, and by 2012 it was bankrupt.

Making it all the more painful is the fact that digital photography was originally invented by Steve Sasson—a Kodak engineer. But Kodak declined to support the new technology. As Sasson recalled to the *New York Times*, management's response was, "That's cute, but don't tell anyone about it." In love with film, company leaders were unimpressed by the earliest version of the new technology, with its low image resolution. In addition, they were simply afraid of cannibalizing their profitable film business—and so failed to consider that they were opening a pathway for other companies to cannibalize it instead.

In short, they succumbed to the gravitational pull of the status quo bias, and, in the words of *The Economist*, found themselves poised, "After 132 years . . . like an old photo, to fade away."

Denial

Denial is a means of pain avoidance. Psychologists tell us that we are motivated by an instinct to avoid pain today, even when this will probably result in a lot more pain tomorrow. Hence our attraction to the denial bias—an instinct that can cause us to make bad decisions that make tomorrow's suffering even more acute.

Take the current threat of catastrophic long-term damage from climate change. The scientific consensus is that unless carbon emissions are radically reduced, changes to the climate—already under way—are likely to be dire and lead to great human suffering. At some critical point, these consequences will become impossible to reverse. Climate scientists differ in their predictions, and there is some uncertainty on the specific timing and levels of carbon in the atmosphere that will represent the point of no return. But the core warning is clear: humanity must act now or risk enormous damage in the future.

Let's step back and reflect on the nature of the challenge posed by the problem of denial. There are two overriding factors to consider:

o   The most important decisions we make in life are those that are irreversible. When faced with a choice that cannot be undone later, it's crucial to think long and hard before determining a course of action.

o   It's sometimes reasonable to accept a risk with minor consequences, especially when there's a countervailing chance of some much greater positive outcome. That's why we happily risk a dollar or two on lottery tickets when a handsome payoff is possible. But when confronted by even a small risk of *major* harm, the rational response is risk mitigation. That's why we take out fire insurance. The likelihood that our home will catch fire is small—but if it did happen, the damage would be devastating.

In the case of climate change, the risks are high, and the potential damage is huge if we allow the problem to escalate. This simple cost/benefit analysis tells us that the logic supporting immediate mitigation measures is overwhelming.

However, mitigation is expensive and inconvenient in the short term. So despite the compelling evidence of potential long-term disaster, many politicians and business leaders, hoping to avoid the short-term pain that might threaten their popularity and power, are resisting the necessary mitigation measures. They justify this position with a range of excuses: "Maybe the scientists are wrong—after all, it's impossible to foresee the future." "Climate has changed in the past without destroying humankind; maybe the next change will be no different." "Perhaps we'll invent some new technology that can reverse the processes that are causing climate change; in the meantime, let's continue with business as usual."

They don't like the burdens of the cure, so they choose to deny the disease.

Siloed Thinking

Organizations are typically organized by function for a good reason: to instill and support the specialized skills required to run the system effectively. But this structure succeeds only when these skills act in combination with each other. In the same way, sports teams require specialists in various positions (the defensive, offensive, and special teams players on an American football squad, for example), but winning requires the orchestration of those skills.

Peter Drucker said the task of a leader is "to get ordinary people to do extraordinary things." That magic happens when we lift each other up through teamwork. A former teammate of Joe Montana, the famed quarterback of the San Francisco 49ers during their glory days of the 1980s, summed up this sentiment concisely: "You know, when Joe was on the team, I played better."

Everyone on a team knows that this is true, at least theoretically. Yet there is a strong tendency for functions to become "tribal," viewing the world through the narrow lens of their own self-interest rather than taking a holistic view of the common good. The results can include lack of coordination, internal dissension, and mistrust. Worst of all, it embeds inside-out thinking, with organizational members viewing their roles solely from their own perspectives rather than seeking to understand the interests and needs of others—especially customers. When an organization becomes a collection of disconnected silos rather than a unified whole, trouble is almost inevitable.

The Blind Men and the Elephant

The Indian parable of the blind men and the elephant neatly captures the dangers of siloed thinking. In ancient times. a group of blind men encountered an elephant for the first time. Touching it from all sides, they tried to determine its nature. Those who contacted the head described the elephant as a water pot, those who felt the ears defined it as a fan, those who touched a leg said it was a tree, and those who felt a tusk thought it was a spear. The blind men fell into arguing amongst themselves, each insisting their vision of the elephant was correct and all the others were wrong. It was only when they listened to each other's perspectives that they were able to construct the whole picture and "see" the elephant as it really was.

The harmful effects of siloed thinking invariably show up in the quality of the customer experience. Too often when we approach a service provider with a problem we want to solve, we get waved off with the answer, "That's not my job." That response amounts to a disservice rather than a service. How pleasing it is to hear instead, "Let me get our team to help you."

To avoid siloed thinking, the only effective remedy is for functions to cooperate in pursuit of a shared purpose. It is the role of strategy to create such unity of action. We'll deal with that topic in a later chapter.

The four biases I've described seldom exist in isolation. While some can be more dominant than others, they often crop up in the same organization, feeding on each other. Without effective countermeasures, they can undermine an organization's ability to base its decisions on objective reality rather than wishful thinking.

Awareness of these often unconscious biases is the essential starting point for addressing them. A good practice is for executive teams to periodically review and discuss each of the biases, perhaps with the help of a skilled facilitator, thereby developing the awareness to recognize and counteract them when they show up. Applying these "mental bulldozers" will substantially enhance an organization's ability to learn effectively.

5. Asking the Right Questions: The Leader's Secret Weapon

If I had 60 minutes to solve a problem, I would spend 55 minutes defining the problem and five minutes thinking about solutions.

ALBERT EINSTEIN

I have stressed the Darwinian logic that the only way to achieve long-term survival is for organizations to practice the art of continuous learning. It is the responsibility of leaders to develop that adaptive capability and serve as the role models. During my time as a CEO, I strived to follow that approach. And now in my career as an educator, I have taken a keen interest in discovering the best learning techniques.

One of the most powerful learning tools I have found is to pose a well-framed question that leads to intense discussion and fresh insights. Like any other skill, doing this well takes lots of practice. Leaders and teachers share at least one trait that can make it tricky for them to become masters of asking questions. Both groups are often regarded as authority figures, expected to know the right answers to everything. This can become intoxicating, and when we are confronted with a difficult question, we may be tempted to uphold our image by guessing. In the end, this benefits no one.

Instead, I have learned the usefulness of simply saying, "I don't know. Let's figure it out together." This honest answer sets the example for authentic inquiry and often leads to fresh discoveries—for both the students and the teacher.

We owe the ancient Greek philosopher Socrates a debt of thanks for demonstrating the power of learning through questions. Before Socrates, roving teachers called Sophists in Greece taught rhetoric, the ability to dazzle your audience with your knowledge in eloquent speeches. Socrates understood the weakness of the Sophists' approach to leadership—the fact that we learn nothing new by repeating what we already know. What's more, an audience retains very little of what is pushed at them without their participation.

Socrates recognized that the acceptance of ignorance is the beginning of wisdom and that we need to interact with others to stimulate mutual learning and arrive at truth. Thus, he turned the way we learn upside-down, replacing oratory with investigative dialogue, a method of mutual discovery we have come to call *the Socratic method.*

Socrates' mother was a midwife, responsible for facilitating the delivery of babies. He saw her profession as a metaphor for his method, explaining, "I don't give birth to ideas, but I facilitate their delivery." He approached questions with intellectual humility, displaying more interest in what's true than in being right.

As a professor, studying Socrates has imbued me with a valuable lesson. My role is not to teach; it is to stimulate learning by serving as an intellectual midwife for the delivery of new insights.

How to Frame Questions That Generate Learning

Everything we have learned through the ages came from a question someone asked. They are our "portals of discovery," to borrow a phrase from novelist James Joyce. The advantage of artfully crafted questions is that they force us to challenge our underlying assumptions, unfreeze our thinking, and open our minds to new perspectives. Moreover, they elicit participation in the learning process, and hence ownership of the resulting insights.

For this reason, the questions we should deploy as leaders are quite different in purpose from the questions deployed in a courtroom. In my prior career as a litigation lawyer, I was drilled in the art of asking effective questions in legal battles. These questions are aimed mainly at testing the honesty of witnesses and exposing evasions or falsehoods. Such courtroom questions are exactly the opposite of learning questions. Litigation is adversarial. Questions in that forum are used as weapons. Learning questions are profoundly different. They are non-threatening invitations to explore an issue jointly and discover insights. No one is on trial. The key is to lead a shared process of exploration that produces mutual benefits, not a win/lose contest.

There's a science to asking questions that are likely to generate real insights. Good questions are *generative*, meaning that they give rise to ideas that didn't exist before.

Asking the wrong question can set off an inquiry in a fruitless direction. Writing in *Forbes* magazine, David Marquet suggests starting questions with "How." As examples:

- o Not "Will we be on time?" But "How likely is it that we will be on time?"
- o Not "Are you sure?" But "How sure are you?"
- o Not "Can we do it?" But "How can we do it?"

Such open-ended questions invite a diagnostic way of assessing an issue rather than a one-word "Yes" or "No" response or, even worse, a defensive attempt at self-justification ("Of course we'll be on time, I promised we would, didn't I?"). I would add that "Why" and "What" questions can do a similar job.

The Question That Won a War

Let's look at how the right question can transform the understanding of a problem and change the course of events.

In 1776, the 13 independent American colonies banded together in a war of independence against the British. George Washington was appointed to lead the colonies' poorly trained, underequipped army against the formidable British forces with their superior skills and greater resources.

Early in the conflict, the American rebel army was close to defeat. The situation looked grim. Washington engaged in an intense debate with his senior officers. "How can we defeat the British?" he asked. They spent hours agonizing over the possibilities from every angle, but could find no good answer. It seemed like a depressing, game-ending conclusion. This was a "How" question, but, given the overwhelming odds they were facing, it was not the best one.

However, this intense debate ultimately gave birth to a transformative question that opened up a totally new way of thinking. Stimulated by the discussion to think more deeply, one of the officers ultimately came up with the right question: "How can we avoid losing?" At first, this reframing might sound defensive, even defeatist. But given the dire circumstances the colonials faced, this back-handed approach proved to be the right one. As they reconsidered the challenge in this new light, the American forces devised an innovative strategy of surprise raids and quick withdrawals to avoid taking losses. Rather than trying to win (against enormous odds), they chose to avoid losing—husbanding their resources and doggedly surviving, gradually wearing down their bigger, stronger opponent.

The strategy worked. They exhausted the British, who eventually withdrew when the entry of the French in support of the Americans provided the final push. It was the right question that saved the day.

The Questions That Define a Democracy

For another example, let's consider the ongoing debate about the essential features of a democracy—a topic with special relevance in today's polarized political climate. Most people describe themselves as supporters of democracy. But what exactly does that mean? How can we define the hallmarks of an effective democracy in a memorable way?

Tony Benn, a British politician, claimed there were five questions to ask people in power that revealed whether a true democracy existed. He often presented these insights when speaking to schoolchildren in the United Kingdom. I don't think there has ever been a better way to boil democracy down to its essence (Figure 5-1).

Benn argued that the last question—"How can we get rid of you?"—is the most important one. In the absence of a consistently observed method for the peaceful transfer of power, democracy is in peril.

ASK THE POWERFUL FIVE QUESTIONS:

1. WHAT POWER HAVE YOU GOT?
2. WHERE DID YOU GET IT FROM?
3. IN WHOSE INTERESTS DO YOU EXERCISE IT?
4. TO WHOM ARE YOU ACCOUNTABLE?
5. HOW CAN WE GET RID OF YOU?

ONLY DEMOCRACY GIVES US THAT RIGHT.

THAT IS WHY NO ONE WITH POWER LIKES DEMOCRACY.

AND THAT IS WHY EVERY GENERATION MUST STRUGGLE TO WIN IT AND KEEP IT --INCLUDING YOU AND ME, HERE AND NOW

TONY BENN

2005

Figure 5.1. Tony Benn's Five Questions
That Define Democracy

The Questions That Help Us Understand the Purpose of a Business

In the business world, there have been competing ideas about the concept of stakeholder primacy. In the past, a common view was that business success was all about serving and pleasing the people who used our products or services. In the words of management guru Peter Drucker, "The purpose of business is to create and keep a customer." In recent decades, this idea was gradually superseded by the philosophy—widely associated with the conservative economist Milton Friedman—that the overriding purpose of a business is to create value for shareholders, on the ground that, after all, they are the owners of the corporation.

One recent volley in the debate came in 2019, when the Business Roundtable produced a statement declaring that the interests of *all* key stakeholders—including customers, shareholders, suppliers, employees, and society at large—should be served. Their rationale was that all these stakeholders are important.

While the Roundtable's expansive view of the purpose of a company is true, I suggest that this formulation misses the main point. I believe that a more helpful approach is to define the key questions that business leaders must ask themselves when setting the strategic direction for their organizations.

For example, when Sam Palmisano was the CEO of IBM, he declared that, in strategic discussions, every IBM executive must produce clear answers to the following four questions:

- o Why should customers choose to do business with us?
- o Why should investors choose to give us their money?
- o Why should employees choose to work in our company?
- o Why should communities in which we work welcome us in their midst?

Palmisano's questions remind us that, in a competitive world, all these stakeholders have choices. The crucial insight is that if any one of these stakeholders is underserved, it undermines a firm's ability to serve the best interests of the others. After all, a business that attracts customers will appeal to investors; creating happy customers requires motivated employees; and bad citizenship will alienate the other three stakeholders.

So the key point is not just that all these stakeholders are important, as the Business Roundtable correctly argued. It is the *mutual interdependence* between them that provides the crucial logic in support of the multi-stake-holder argument.

The Question That Changed
Starbucks' Strategy

Even a single penetrating question can generate insights that will improve a company's competitive thinking. Starbucks' mission statement says, "We are not in the coffee business serving people. We are in the people business serving coffee."

This definition has sparked questions that have led to concrete, positive changes in the behavior of Starbucks' employees. For example, in the company's early years, employees would call out the name of your drink when it was ready. Then, in 2011, a curious barista began pondering the question, "What goes to the heart of being a people business?" This line of inquiry inspired him to write the names of customers by hand on cups to personalize the experience, and to call out the customer names rather than the names of drinks.

It turned out that customers loved this. After all, how often does an item you purchase come with your name on it? The idea traveled to headquarters and was quickly adopted as standard practice. Today, customers' names appear on a printed label on their cups four billion times a year at 30,000 Starbucks locations worldwide.

As this example shows, customer satisfaction is not just about product performance; it is also about how it makes people *feel*. The essential ingredient is *empathy*—seeing the world through the eyes of the customer. Market research is not enough. The Starbucks barista demonstrated how asking thoughtful questions can make the difference.

The Questions That Made Flying Safer

A powerful set of questions is employed by the U.S. military in its famed After Action Review (AAR) system. The AAR is a rigorous inquiry conducted after every military engagement (simulated or real) to elicit lessons learned. This action-learning process focuses on four questions:

o   What was meant to happen?
o   What actually happened?
o   Why did it happen?
o   How can we do better in future?

The process focuses on learning, not blaming. The insights collected are sent to the Center for Army Lessons Learned (CALL), then shared throughout the army's ranks worldwide.

The U.S. airline industry was inspired by the power of this method. After a series of fatal crashes in the mid-1990s, the Federal Aviation Administration (FAA) established a voluntary no-blame incident reporting system. The AAR method is applied to identify the root causes of every near-miss or crash, and the resulting insights are disseminated throughout the industry. Because of this learning system, flying now becomes safer after every mishap.

The results have been remarkable. In the 14 years after the FAA created the system, U.S. airlines carried more than eight billion passengers—the equivalent of the world's population—without a single fatal accident.

The Question That Could Have Improved Covid Outcomes

When broad public compliance is required to prevent the transmission of an infectious disease, asking the right questions becomes critical in devising an effective policy. According to the *New York Times* columnist Ezra Klein, the United States failed this test when managing the spread of Covid-19. In an opinion piece on February 6, 2022, he stated flatly, "We began this pandemic by asking the wrong questions, and thus got the wrong answers."

Klein went on to explain. In a survey of 195 countries, the United States had ranked number one in pandemic preparedness. It had all the necessary tools and policy recommendations in place: masking, social distancing, vaccinations, testing, and so on. Yet despite government urging, the public response to the advent of Covid-19 was divided along ideological lines, leading to poor outcomes. The United States had 545 coronavirus cases per 1,000 residents. By contrast, Canada had 346, Germany 188, and Japan only 67.

Why did the United States perform so poorly despite being the best prepared? Klein argues that the main reason lies in a key finding in the survey: the United States had the lowest possible score on public confidence in government combined with high social divisiveness. In Japan, on the other hand, where case rates were eight times lower, citizens have high trust in government and high social solidarity. They were given simple rules and followed them willingly.

Klein concludes that American public health authorities were asking the wrong question: "How can we achieve compliance in the face of resistance?" This question led to policies that simply inflamed emotions and intensified resistance. The right question, he says, would have been, "What does good pandemic policy look like for a low-trust, individualistic society?" This framing could have produced a clearer definition of the underlying problem to be solved—and better choices by policy makers.

As these examples illustrate, leaders can facilitate the creation of new ideas and encourage learning by promoting the ability to ask the right questions throughout their organizations. Good questions help us solve complex problems. Even more important is their generative capacity, which enables us to open our minds to ideas that didn't exist before.

Socrates gave us a powerful new way of thinking 2,500 years ago. Today, his ideas are more timely than ever. In this disruptive age, leaders must heed his most important lesson: We will never have all the right answers, but we must have the right questions.

**Seven Important Questions We Seldom Ask
Before Making a Decision**

- What assumptions must be true for this to be the right decision?
- What will be the consequences of *not* taking this decision?
- What are we aiming to achieve and how will we measure success?
- What is the strongest counter-argument to taking this decision?
- If we were not already in this business, would we enter it now?
- What is the problem to be solved in the eyes of the customer?
- What do we care about beyond making money?

6. The Truth Sprouts Everywhere: The Wisdom of the Elders

Those who respect the elderly pave
their own road toward success.

AFRICAN PROVERB

W e are all, to a significant extent, a product of our histories. My own formative years took place in South Africa, where I was born and raised. As I collected my thoughts for this book, my mind often traveled back to the various "disturbances" in those early years that helped shape who I am.

I grew up in a medium-sized coastal town called East London in a tight-knit family of four. I would become the only member of our family to go to college. My older sister, Phoebe, was a clever, conscientious girl who invariably came first in her class. My parents couldn't afford to send us both to college, and Phoebe's grades would have made her a likely choice. But Phoebe insisted that this right belonged to me as the male sibling and thus the likely breadwinner for my future family. I have always felt grateful to her for this act of self-sacrifice and the way she championed me.

My father was a station master on the South African Railways, which meant he wore a uniform. As a small boy, I was impressed by the air of authority this conveyed. It made my father seem comparable in importance to another high-ranking civilian wearing a uniform—the chief constable, who wielded the power of law and order in our community. My father was far too humble to see it that way. But he was an imperturbable, steadfast man who lived by the simple virtue of always standing up for the right thing, and over time this basic, rock-solid integrity became his true source of authority in my mind.

My mother was a homemaker, an outstanding seamstress, and a wonderful cook. With her bright mind, ready laugh, and insatiable curiosity, her personality was in many ways the opposite of my father's, but they operated well as a team.

She was somewhat protective of me. Each day, as I left for school, she would call out after me, "Do you have a clean handkerchief?" A clean handkerchief in my pocket is a habit I have followed to this day.

The Grip of Mental Imprinting

I've written in these pages about the awful effect of apartheid on the people of South Africa. During my formative years, the fact of racial segregation was a foundational reality imprinted on my mind. I viewed it as normal, simply part of the way the world worked. I had no frame of reference to tell me otherwise. This social norm was reinforced by all the authority figures in my life, from my parents and teachers to our civic leaders. Added to this, the philosophy of racial segregation was endorsed by the hugely influential Dutch Reformed Church, which preached that this was part of God's divine purpose.

LEADERSHIP—THE INSIDE STORY

Like most white families in South Africa, we had Black servants—a full-time house maid and a gardener who came once a week to mow the lawn. My parents taught me to treat them, and all Black people, with respect and kindness, and my all-boys, all-white school similarly emphasized courtesy towards all as a part of its character-building mission.

However, these guidelines operated within the controlling structure of a segregated society. The whites harbored a comforting sense of self-justification on the ground that the Blacks were "free" to build their own lives in their own areas according to their own culture. But the reality was that the lives of Black South Africans were strictly limited by the rules of a hierarchical system in which whites were to Blacks as parents to children. The condescending mental construct that persisted from colonial times was that our mission was to "civilize" the Blacks, who should feel grateful for this contribution to their development.

This ethos expressed itself in the verbal interactions between the races. Blacks were not referred to as "women" or "men," but as "girls" and "boys," regardless of their age. I often overheard white adults saying, "I wish I could find a more hardworking girl," or "We have an excellent garden boy." Blacks, on the other hand, addressed white males as "baas" (Afrikaans for "boss") and white females as "madam" even when they were not in the employ of the person they were speaking to. In my preteen years, I was called "basie" or small boss, even (absurdly) by elderly Black men and women. Then as a teenager, I graduated to "baas." This language implicitly reinforced the idea of Black inferiority.

Unlearning: The Key to Thinking in New Ways

What does it take to overcome the biases that flow from this kind of deeply embedded mental imprinting? Author and futurist Alvin Toffler famously described the challenge we face in a rapidly changing world as the need to learn, unlearn, and relearn. Whenever I ask executive groups which of these three behaviors is the hardest to master, a chorus of agreement comes back: "unlearn." That applies with special force to the biases we imbibe as children—assumptions about the world so deeply ingrained in our minds that we scarcely notice them, let alone think to question them.

Luckily, as I grew up, I was presented with the disturbances necessary to begin unlearning my childhood biases. The change didn't happen instantly; instead, it occurred through a slow-moving yet profound journey of discovery.

My uncle Colin and aunt Lizzie owned a farm a two-hour drive from East London. During school holidays, I was often sent to the farm to play with my cousins and benefit from the country air. My aunt and uncle had seven children—four boys and three girls. I became the eighth child, and this mob of children created a rather unruly and boisterous atmosphere. My Aunt Lizzie served as the general manager of the entire farming enterprise and ran the place (including my uncle) like General Patton. A large staff of household and farm workers provided the support system.

Wisdom from Humble Teachers

Emerging from this melee was a figure that made a lasting impression on me—the head housemaid, a remarkable, matriarchal Black woman called Nomaquala. (This is my phonetic spelling of her name, which I never saw written down.) She was the Mother Teresa to Aunt Lizzie's General Patton.

A short, ample, jovial woman with a personality larger than her frame, Nomaquala was the friend and confidant of all the children. She knew our individual preferences and foibles and was our constant source of advice and encouragement. If you scraped your knee, were being treated unfairly, or felt sick, you went to Nomaquala for comfort or first aid. She made every child feel valued and special. She knew everyone's favorite foods, so when I arrived at the farm for the holidays, she would clap her hands with joy and point to the stove where pancakes, which I loved, were already frying in the pan. "Wow, you have grown so much since last time," she would exclaim approvingly.

Nomaquala and I became close. While my cousins, who were schooled in the hardy ways of farm life, would sometimes scoff at me for being a bookish "townie," she would ask about my school marks and heap praise on me for my achievements. She embraced the superstition that sea water had curative powers, so I always brought her a small bottle of water from the seashore near my home, which she secretly kept in her hut.

As Namaquala grew older, she confided in me about her dream of seeing the sea before she died. She often asked me to describe it. Groping for a comparison, I told her to think about the dam on the farm, where you could see the opposite bank. "The sea is so big that you can't see the other side," I told her. It was not easy for her to visualize this.

Eventually, my uncle agreed to allow my cousin Henry and me to borrow his car to drive Nomaquala to glimpse the sea in my hometown. This was a momentous occasion for her, and her excitement grew as we neared our destination. It was a bright, sunny day as we got out of the car and led her to the railings overlooking the Indian Ocean with its huge waves pounding the rocks below. Her jaw dropped.

"Do you see now how big it is?" I asked her.

"Yes," she replied, "but it moves!" Her biggest revelation was seeing the incessant waves, a feature I had never thought to mention. "What makes it move?" she asked.

"The moon," I replied.

Nomaquala just laughed. She'd never had a formal education, so no one had ever explained to her about the tides.

But while she was not versed in the intricacies of science, her homespun wisdom was unequaled.

On the drive back to the farm, Nomaquala was deep in thought. Eventually, she posed her big question. "If the moon is so strong that it can make the big ocean move, why doesn't it make our small dam at the farm move, too?"

Henry and I glanced at each other to see who could answer. We were both stumped. "I'll have to ask my teacher," I told her.

Prompted by my friendship and admiration for Nomaquala, I began to have quiet conversations with other farm workers who could speak some English. Sometimes I sat and listened while the elders gathered in a circle to discuss their tribal affairs and dilemmas—for example, how to deal with a difficult child, how to resolve an interpersonal conflict, or the best way to console someone in pain and near death. I was awed by the wisdom that had been passed on through the generations by word of mouth about the natural world, human affairs, and life's most difficult problems. I was struck by their patient deliberations and their practice of listening intently to one another as they reached for consensus. My attitude of condescension towards African people was gradually replaced by admiration for what they could teach us all about life and living it well. This experience helped me to see an important connection. Our personal philosophy and the way we lead are woven into the same cloth.

We tend to think the great contributions in philosophy were generated mainly by the Greeks, Romans, and Eastern sages, then supplemented by the so-called Enlightenment thinkers of the seventeenth and eighteenth centuries. But the wisdom passed down by the tribal elders in Africa is just as profound, even though it is not encapsulated in any impressive written tome or taught in university classes. I will be forever grateful for its contribution to my own learning.

As a tribute to that legacy, I would like to share with you some of my favorite African proverbs. Each is a simple-sounding statement that repays repeated readings with gradually deepening insight into important facets of our life on this Earth—insights that any leader may find valuable.

If you want to go fast, go alone. If you want to go far, go together.

I am because you are.

When the music changes, so does the dance.

When an elder dies, a library burns to the ground.

If you close your eyes to facts, you will learn through accidents.

What counts is not the number of seeds you scatter. It's the number of seeds you nurture.

Only a fool tests the depth of the water with both feet.

Don't look where you fell. Look where you slipped.

7. Taking a Walk: A Pathway to Breakthrough Ideas

Angels whisper to a man when he goes for a walk.

RAYMOND INMON

D uring my years as a CEO based in New York City, I developed a daily habit. Every morning before work, I walked for two miles through Central Park. My initial motivation was physical fitness, but I soon made a discovery: during these walks, new ideas would come to me totally unbidden. Often, I found a solution to a knotty problem that had defied my attempts to produce a good answer through prior analysis.

I came to realize that these solo walks were not just a form of physical exercise; they induced a state of mental freedom that released creative avenues of thought not generated in formal processes of discovery. I began protecting my walking time zealously. On overseas business trips, the rule was that my daily schedule would not begin until I had done my two-mile walk. Among my favorite places were the scenic botanical gardens in Sydney and the tranquil water gardens in Tokyo. Settings like these intensified my awareness of our human connections to the natural world, and these "disturbances" opened my mind to broader perspectives. Colleagues took to teasing me when I offered a fresh idea during a meeting: "Ah, we see you took your walk this morning!"

The Science Behind the Magic of Walking

What was going on here? At first, I thought this experience was idiosyncratic, a personal quirk. But I soon learned that science tells a different story. The process of walking improves our cognitive function by releasing two chemicals: A protein called BDNF that nourishes and energizes our neurons, and hormones known as endorphins that produce a sense of calm and well-being.

The combination of these chemical actions enables us to think in deeper, more imaginative ways. This appears to be true for virtually everyone. A Stanford study released in 2014 found that walking increased a person's "creative output" by an average of 60 percent. Steve Jobs of Apple was known for conducting walking meetings, which are increasingly popular among employers, as highlighted in a front-page article of the *Wall Street Journal* that quoted an executive enthusing about how "ideas started to come to life" during a walk-and-talk through Bryant Park in midtown Manhattan.

Many of the world's great thinkers got their breakthrough ideas while walking:

o   James Watt, who perfected the steam engine that ushered in the railroad system, came upon his discovery while going for a Sunday walk. He relates, "I was thinking upon the engine at the time and had gone as far as the Herd's house when the idea came into my mind."

o Nikola Tesla gave birth to the idea of the rotating magnetic field that enabled broad-scale electrification during a walk in a Budapest park in 1882.

o Friedrich Nietzsche, the 19th-century philosopher, produced his most profound thoughts during long alpine walks. "All truly great thoughts are conceived while walking," he claimed.

o Ludwig van Beethoven, the renowned composer, took long walks in the afternoons, regardless of the weather. He carried a pen and sheets of paper on which he recorded his many inspirations during these outings.

o Werner Heisenberg, who discovered the foundations of quantum physics, achieved the breakthrough in his thinking during a two-week absence from the University of Göttingen to recover from an illness. He traveled alone to a remote archipelago on the North Sea and was doing nothing but taking daily walks and going for long swims. During these activities, the intricacies of quantum theory formed clearly in his mind.

Today's business environment presents us with a bewildering mixture of speed and complexity. It is becoming nearly impossible to make sense of these confusing conditions with traditional thinking tools. We are being forced into shaping the future of our organizations on the run. We call hasty meetings, glance quickly at position papers, sit through dense PowerPoint presentations, and are then expected to make immediate decisions. I often hear the troubling comment from executives that "We don't have time to do a strategy." The challenge is clear: We must develop better cognitive skills to cope with a disruptive landscape. Walking is surprisingly effective in helping us develop these skills.

There are essentially two modes of thinking: breaking an issue down into its component pieces (analysis) and seeing how the pieces fit together (synthesis). While analysis can deepen our understanding of an issue, synthesis provides contextual intelligence through our ability to recognize interconnected patterns. Research shows that strong analytical skills are common among executives, whereas the ability to synthesize is very rare.

This presents a problem. Many of the most important advancements in knowledge, such as Einstein's theory of relativity and Darwin's insights on evolution, have been acts of synthesis rather than analysis. They involve seeing connections that had previously not been understood. By now, it should be no surprise to hear that Charles Darwin took regular walks. Einstein, while he was grappling with the complexities of his general theory, induced his mind to wander by playing Mozart on his violin.

As these examples show, to walk is to invite thinking, and to do so in different, more creative ways than those we usually employ. I have found on my walks that most of my insights were acts of synthesis rather than analysis—finding meaning in the relationship between things. This helps us make sense out of chaos which is a crucial role of strategic thinking.

Two classical images sum up the contrasts in thinking methods. The first is Rodin's *The Thinker* (Figure 7-1). It is an exquisite depiction of the male form in a contemplative mode, but it sends a misleading message. A static posture is not the best way to develop creative ideas.

The second image, from Raphael's painting *The School of Athens*, shows Plato and Aristotle walking and reasoning together (Figure 7-2). This captures Aristotle's unique practice of teaching while walking about. His followers became known as the *peripatetics,* from the Greek word for "strolling around."

Figure 7.1. *The Thinker,* Rodin

Figure 7.2. *The School of Athens* (detail), Raphael

Aristotle's great example has come full circle. Modern times have created daunting challenges of thinking clearly in chaotic conditions while being assailed by constant distractions. Winning strategies depend on our ability to see through the fog of complexity and develop the keenest insights. For this to happen, we need to create the right mental conditions. A simple and effective method is within our grasp. Become a peripatetic. In today's parlance, take a hike.

Finally, a confession, and you have probably already guessed it: many of the ideas in this book were formed during my morning walks.

Tips for Walking as a Creative Practice

o Walk as a daily habit. Mornings are best.

o Venture outdoors (weather permitting) so you are exposed to the wider world.

o Turn off your cell phone.

o Ideally, walk for 20 to 30 minutes. Also take brief walks between intense mental tasks.

o Free up your mind. Ideas will come to you.

o Write down your insights afterwards in a learning journal.

8. Getting Information to Flow from the Bottom Up

If I had to reduce the responsibilities of a good follower to a single rule, it would be to speak truth to power.

WARREN BENNIS

I n military campaigns, success is crucially dependent on the swift and accurate flow of information from the front lines to the command centers. The same is true in a business. A company's competitive battles happen on the ground, not in the executive suite. Therefore, the most current and actionable source of marketplace intelligence is that which flows from the bottom of the organization up to the leaders at the top. When the communication conduit from the bottom up is blocked, organizations face a survival problem.

Unfortunately, many companies are not addressing this priority. When conducting leadership seminars, I regularly ask participants to define their company's biggest barriers to success. Disturbingly often, I hear that the main impediment is their top leaders' immunity to feedback. "They just won't listen to new ideas," one participant says. "They are living in yesterday's world," says another. "They think they have it all figured out and simply want us to execute," comments a third.

When I first heard such complaints, my initial reaction was to place responsibility on the participants themselves. I pointed out that effective leaders are skilled at influencing in three directions: down, up, and across. Therefore, we should all see ourselves as leading from the middle, regardless of our status. Leading up, by providing valuable feedback to those above you, is an essential skill for leaders at every level, but one that is sorely neglected.

There is no "they" in leadership, I argued. The question: "Why don't they . . ." will produce no results except a sense of victimhood. "You simply have to be better at leading up," I declared.

All of these observations were correct. However, in wrestling repeatedly with this challenge, I have come to realize that, while subordinates do indeed have a key role in pushing their leaders in the right direction, they cannot achieve this on their own. Their bosses need to be willing participants in leading up; indeed, they need to champion the practice.

Overcoming the Curse of Power

This is easier said than done. During my 20 years as a CEO, I had many occasions to reflect on the dangers of what I call "the curse of power." They takes two forms. First, as we rise to higher positions in a hierarchy, we become increasingly more isolated from what is happening at ground level. Second, there is a natural tendency for subordinates to tell you what they think you want to hear. In the absence of effective antidotes to these two tendencies, leaders can become blind to truth. This behavior sets a negative example that infects the entire organization.

One episode sticks in my memory. One day, my CFO came into my office to brief me on a problem that had been festering for about three months. Over time, it had become much harder to solve.

"Why didn't someone tell me earlier?" I asked in frustration.

"Willie," he replied, "sometimes we find you a little intimidating."

For the first time, I realized that my own attitude was discouraging open feedback. Candidly, I didn't feel I was intimidating, nor was I trying to be—but this was the impression I'd created. I realized how ignorant we can be about our own blind spots. Closing the door, I asked for examples of my negative behavior, which the CFO willingly provided. It didn't happen often—perhaps mainly when I was in a bad mood—but the examples cited were enough to deter people from delivering unpleasant news to me.

At our next executive committee meeting, we spent time discussing the challenge of promoting upward feedback and hashed out an operating policy to embed this practice in the firm's culture. And of course I made an effort to avoid repeating the intimidating behaviors that had helped block the communication channels in the first place.

Dr. Ash Tewari, the pioneering surgeon I mentioned in chapter two, diligently practices this type of interactive feedback with his team. During his regular insight-sharing sessions, everyone rapidly gets to know and adopt the best medical practices everyone else has learned. Tewari himself is the keenest learner on the team, and to ensure the learning never stops, he insists on treating everyone around him as an equal source of insight. Tewari combats the curse of power by insisting that learning demands "no subordination."

Not surprisingly, a Gallup poll showed that companies that are not good at listening to their employees are substantially less successful than their competitors. It's not hard to find examples that illustrate the harm done.

Consider the travails of the Boeing corporation arising from the design flaws of the 737 MAX airliner, which caused two fatal crashes, one in Indonesia and one in Ethiopia, in 2018 and 2019. During the ensuing investigations, it became clear that several engineers close to the design of the aircraft had seen the problems and voiced concern about the potential consequences. But the stark reality of impending disaster failed to reach the top leaders, who were preoccupied with cost and timing issues, until too late in the process.

As a result, Boeing experienced a massive hit to its profitability, as well as reputational damage that, sadly, appears all too well deserved. Quality issues have continued to plague the company. In January 2024, a door panel on a 737 MAX 9 blew open mid-flight, causing panic among the passengers. Miraculously, no one was killed. But the subsequent investigation showed that three essential bolts were missing from the door plug, raising questions about quality control practices in Boeing's production plants.

It's impossible to predict when the weaknesses of a flawed management culture will come back to bite you—but eventually they will, with consequences that can be devastating. Discouraging the delivery of timely information to top leadership—or ignoring the messages once they are delivered—is a dangerous flaw that can undermine an organization's effectiveness.

Organizations Need a New Social Contract

Leading up, then, is urgently needed. But it's extraordinarily difficult to practice. It's fraught with psychological sensitivities, questions of loyalty, and perceived challenges to authority. In view of these complications, success requires a reset of cultural norms—a new social contract, if you like—deliberately designed to promote open communication in both directions.

At the start of each new hierarchical relationship, the parties need to sit down and have a candid discussion about how they will work together. Subordinates should explicitly seek permission to provide upward feedback, so that this doesn't occur by surprise or in ways that are perceived as inappropriate. In the best of all worlds, bosses would themselves initiate this discussion. Even in existing relationships, it is a good idea for this kind of conversation to take place periodically.

An upward feedback session should never be framed as a challenge to authority or an expression of disloyalty. And a subordinate should always avoid offering any suggestion designed to promote a personal agenda (to undermine an internal rival, for example). This motive invariably reveals itself and destroys the trust necessary for mutual learning. The only agenda should be sharing ideas to promote the long-term success of the organization. This process should be socialized through organization-wide practices.

Leading Up with "Divine Discontent"

I think of the great example set by David Ogilvy, the founder of the global advertising company Ogilvy and Mather (now part of the global WPP Group). Every year, Ogilvy would convene a gathering that brought together company executives from every part of the world. In his keynote speech, he always stressed the need for sharing ideas across boundaries and upwards so that their clients in every country could expect to receive the best ideas from O&M globally, not just locally. He exhorted his organization to practice what he called "divine discontent"—to identify what was not working well, always accompanied by a recommendation on how to do it better.

This is good advice on how to do upward feedback. I know from experience how dispiriting it feels to hear complaints from subordinates without suggestions on how to solve the problem.

Leading up is not easy. But we have a duty to help each other learn and grow, regardless of rank. We all have our blind spots. When I look back on my corporate career, the subordinates I valued most were those who helped me improve as a leader through their honest feedback—even when it was painful at the time.

The burden of leading our leaders is a shared one. Bosses must set the example by issuing the invitation for honest feedback from below and by being willing to learn from it. Subordinates, in turn, should respond to that invitation with candor and thoughtfulness. For them, the golden rules are expressing "divine discontent" and practicing the courageous act of telling truth to power.

9. Creating a Winning Strategy: Learning at the Speed of Change

We need a philosophy of strategy that contains
the seeds of its constant rejuvenation—
a way to chart strategy in an unstable environment.

CARL VON CLAUSEWITZ

S trategic leadership—one of the three domains of leadership I described in chapter one—is the way organizations create their future by establishing their competitive advantage and their key priorities for success. It's a high-stakes activity, yet few managers know what constitutes strategic thinking. The result is that strategy is widely misunderstood and misapplied. To meet today's challenges, prevailing ways of creating a strategy need a radical overhaul.

Static Methods No Longer Work

Many companies develop a strategy only sporadically, when they want to solve a particular problem—to go from point A to point B. This ad-hoc, one-and-done approach to strategy is no longer adequate. Today's marketplace is more dynamic than ever, demanding a process of learning and regeneration that is continuous. As the humorist Will Rogers admonished us, "It's no good being on the right track. If you just sit there, you'll be run over."

Consider the fate of Nokia and Blackberry after the introduction of Apple's iPhone in 2007. Both had previously held dominant positions in the mobile phone market and probably thought they had it made. Even Barack Obama, when assuming the presidency in early 2009, joked about the data security rules he had to follow by saying, "As long as they don't take my Blackberry away." Nevertheless, in short order, not only Obama's Blackberry but the millions of other Blackberries in use would begin to disappear, replaced by the new smart phones with attractive touch screens and revolutionary access to a world of apps. Apple was simply better than its rivals at tuning in to customer preferences, making Nokia and Blackberry obsolete with startling speed.

Today (early 2024), we are seeing the genesis of another technology disruption. After years of R&D work in backroom labs, Chat GPT, a generative AI tool from Open AI, was launched in November 2022. It quickly captured the imagination of the world through its ability to solve problems and respond, seemingly intelligently, to questions in narrative form. Chat GPT reached 100 million active users within just two months after its launch, making it the fastest growing consumer application in history. By comparison, TikTok, the second fastest, took nine months to reach that level.

Like many new technologies, AI creates possible dangers. Achieving the great promise of AI without incurring its potentially harmful effects presents individual leaders, organizations, and governments alike with an unprecedented test of learning and adaptation. But the long-term effect is likely to be the emergence of new, AI-powered digital platforms facilitating transformational improvements in business and personal productivity and the emergence of new winners and losers. Once again, the strategic landscape will have been reordered for countless businesses, all with little advance warning.

This kind of volatility in today's economic universe poses a huge challenge for leaders, whose ultimate duty is to ensure the sustainability of the enterprises they run. Some have argued that in a marketplace roiled by disruptions such as these, the goal of sustainable competitive advantage is no longer achievable. I disagree. It is true that the advantages delivered by specific products and services are often overtaken by events. But the duty of sustainability has not gone away. It's the process for achieving it that's broken.

A New Approach to Strategy

The time has come for us to reinvent the way strategy does its job. Let's start by considering the fundamental nature of the task.

Just like organisms in nature, organizations are bound by the Darwinian laws of evolutionary success. These dictate that survival depends on the ability to generate favorable variations that are best adapted to the changing environment.

Take the example of antibiotics. They became something of a magic bullet after World War II through their ability to vanquish a wide range of bacterial diseases that had been the scourge of mankind. But now many of these therapies have begun to meet resistance from so-called superbugs, bacteria that have evolved ways of evading the potency of antibiotics. The *Lancet* medical journal has estimated that in 2019 antibiotic resistance was responsible for over a million deaths. This number is rising, and there is now a frightening likelihood that the golden era of antibiotics is gradually ending. The reason is simple: bacteria are faster at adapting than antibiotics.

When your enemy is dynamic and you are static, you will lose the evolutionary battle for survival. Realizing this unequal contest, medical researchers are now racing to find viruses that are capable of killing bacteria. The advantage of viruses is their flexibility: unlike chemical antibiotics, they can evolve as fast as their prey. Perhaps such viruses will give humans an edge in the next round of the never-ending struggle for survival.

Let's apply these universal lessons to human systems. Like organisms in nature, organizations are born, grow to maturity, and eventually decline and die. Some die young, while others last for an astonishingly long time. But here's the thing: the lifespan of an organization is not a function of its age. It is a function of its adaptive capacity. And that, in turn, is driven by learning. This logic is the single most important idea in this book.

The Strategic Learning Process

How, then, can leaders instill this kind of adaptive capacity in their organizations? It won't happen simply through exhortation. The required learning must be built into the fabric of how an organization develops and renews its strategies. Therefore, what the practice of strategy needs is a process revolution—a shift of gear from strategy as planning to strategy as learning.

In service of this goal, I have created a practical process called Strategic Learning, that is designed to heed the Darwinian imperative by creating an enterprise capable of ongoing learning and renewal in response to changing conditions (Figure 9-1). The process involves four steps that move in a cycle:

- o **Learn** through a situation analysis to create insights into the external environment and your own realities.
- o **Focus** by using these insights to make choices on where you will compete and by defining your winning proposition and key priorities.
- o **Align** by mobilizing your business system and motivating your people in support your chosen strategy.
- o **Execute** better and faster than your competitors.

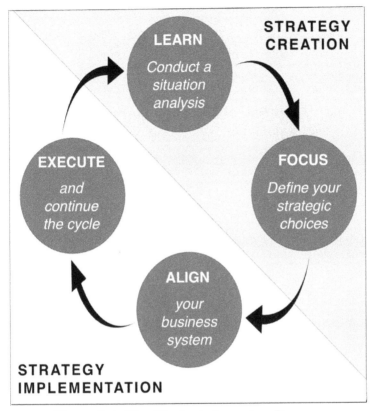

Figure 9.1. The Strategic Learning Process

Then you loop back to the Learn step, thus creating a cycle of ongoing learning and adaptation.

Following the right sequence is crucial. The rule of the road is that intelligence precedes operations and structure follows strategy. The essential starting point is the situation analysis; the intelligence system informs all the subsequent steps.

The elements do not work in isolation. The power of the process comes from the elements working together as a mutually reinforcing system. The linkages are just as important as the outputs.

Note that the process is outside-in. Success occurs outside the boundaries of an organization, not inside. As Darwin reminded us, our survival depends on our ability to adapt to the external environment. The external environment won't do us the favor of adapting to us. That's why outside-in thinking is the essential discipline of any successful strategy.

The Focus step is the heart of a strategy. This involves making the best choices on how to mobilize our limited resources to achieve competitive advantage. These choices boil down to answering three key questions:

- ○ Where—in which industries, markets, and geographies—will we compete?
- ○ What will be our winning proposition? That is, what unique benefits will we offer our customers that gives them a compelling reason to choose us over the competition?
- ○ What will be our key priorities for success?

Without clear and concrete answers to these questions, an organization cannot claim to have a strategy, and its decisions will be scattered and directionless.

Strategy Is About Winning

As we think about our organization's winning proposition we must confront the reality that customers have choices, and they make their choices with reference to the alternatives available to them. Therefore, the central question is, "Why should customers choose to do business with you?"

Some companies believe that defining a "value proposition" suffices to answer this question. I suggest this formulation misses the mark. All value is relative. In a competitive world, absolute definitions of value have no meaning. Winning means offering a *measurable margin of difference* in the value we offer our customers. In Darwinian terms, this is an organization's *favorable variation*. It's all about differentiation.

My favorite weekly magazine is *The Economist*. It defines its winning proposition in stark, galvanizing terms: "We *explain* the world to our readers." Its distinguishing attribute is summed up in that single word "explain." Reporting the news is straightforward; explaining it for those trying to make sense of complex events and understand their implications is where the extra value lies. That is hard to do, but *The Economist* stays true to this singular mission.

And in a wink to its readers, it adds the slogan: "Great minds like a think." *The Economist* is successful largely because of its crystal-clear differentiating proposition.

The remarkable success of Amazon's online retail business offers us another good example of effective differentiation. It defines its winning proposition as follows: "We make it easy for people to buy things by offering a wide range of products with great prices and fast delivery."

Again, this is expressed in simple language and serves both as a rallying cry for Amazon's employees and a compelling proposition for its customers. Note that Amazon does not sell a single unique product. You can buy exactly the same products at any mass merchandiser wherever you may reside. Amazon's margin of difference lies in its service model—the way it treats its customers and makes them feel.

We must remember that the Strategic Learning cycle is continuous, always looping back to the Learn step. As the U.S. Army War College emphasizes, strategy is a process of continuous assessment and re-assessment in the face of constantly changing conditions.

Innovation Never Stops

Sometimes, business leaders believe that they don't need to engage in a process of renewal like Strategic Learning. A company leader may say to me, "Our industry is mature. The products and services we offer have become commoditized, and all of the companies in the marketplace have become the same. Now we must compete on price and protect our profit margins through cost reductions." To succumb to this philosophy is to abandon the pursuit of value creation. With ingenuity, there is virtually always an opportunity to achieve differentiation, and a good situation analysis should uncover those ideas. In fact, I believe that, with rare exceptions, there is no such thing as a commodity. At either end of any transaction are human beings with needs and preferences—and by delving deeply into those needs and preferences, it should be possible to find a way to offer customers something unique and valuable, as Amazon has done.

A good example is the U.S. yogurt industry. By 2005, it had settled into maturity with modest growth and little innovation aside from variations in flavor, fat content, and packaging that made only incremental differences. One variety, known as Greek yogurt, made up a meager one percent of the market and seemed to be dead in the water.

But that year, a Turkish immigrant named Hamdi Ulukaya, who'd worked as a shepherd in his homeland, launched a new Greek yogurt called Chobani (meaning "shepherd" in Turkish). It differentiated itself by emphasizing its quality, authenticity, and social conscience. The brand hit a nerve with customers. In a stunning coup, the launch disrupted the once-stable yogurt market. Chobani overtook Yoplait as the market leader, and within ten years it reached over $2 billion in revenue. In the process, the Greek yogurt segment surged to over 50 percent of the total market.

Strategic Learning is now a central part of the way we teach strategy in Columbia's Executive Education programs. It has also been widely adopted as a core process by many organizations in both the commercial and nonprofit spheres, often with transformative results.

I sometimes get asked whether Strategic Learning is a sure-fire method for business success. The evidence shows it can be a powerful tool. But, like any business process, it is an enabler, not a guarantee. Leaders themselves are the difference-makers. Of course, the method involves following certain disciplines, but it is less a mechanical activity than a way of thinking. As military strategist Carl von Clausewitz said, "What matters most is not *what* we have thought, but *how* we have thought it." Strategic Learning offers a system of thinking that can help you achieve the combination of focus and the adaptive capacity you need for ongoing success.[*]

Above all, remember this: the external environment will not stand still for us. Therefore, winning once is not enough; we must go on winning. To achieve the goal of sustainability, leaders should apply a method like Strategic

---

[*] For more information on how to apply the Strategic Learning method, readers are invited to visit my website: www.williepietersen.com.

Learning on a continuous basis so that their organizations are geared to learn at the speed of change.

10. Setting Priorities:
Why Five Is the Wrong Number

Things that matter most must never be
at the mercy of things that matter least.

GOETHE

A s I emphasized in the prior chapter, strategy is about winning—which is why it's so crucial for an organization to clearly define its winning proposition. But a winning proposition without the right priorities to direct the organization's scarce resources is like a performance car without a steering wheel (a striking metaphor I've borrowed from journalist Thomas E. Ricks).* And prioritization is hard work, demanding a skill that is crucial but rare: the ability to distinguish the important from the unimportant.

Carl von Clausewitz, mentioned in the last chapter, was a Prussian general who fought against Napoleon. Published in 1835, *On War,* his classic guide to military strategy, offers precepts that remain widely taught in military schools and are highly relevant to the modern business strategist.

Clausewitz gave us this powerful definition of strategy: "The talent of the strategist is to identify the decisive point and to concentrate everything on it, removing forces from secondary fronts and ignoring lesser objectives."

Let's unpack Clausewitz's definition by examining its key words:

---

* *First Principles: What America's Founders Learned from the Greeks and Romans and How That Shaped Our Country* by Thomas E. Ricks (New York: Harper, 2020).

o "The decisive point": Here Clausewitz refers to what I call the winning proposition—the core idea defining how we will create competitive advantage.

o "Concentrate everything on it": Note especially the word "everything," chosen to show that Clausewitz meant not only our physical resources but also the hearts, minds, and energies of our people. To quote the military historian Basil Hart, "All the lessons of war can be reduced to a single word: concentration."

o "Removing forces from secondary fronts": Relentlessly eliminate everything that does not directly support the winning proposition and the key priorities it dictates.

o "Ignoring lesser objectives": Don't allow the incessant steam of distractions to weaken your focus; permit no sideshows. Always keep the main thing the main thing.

Success, in other words, is all about focus, concentration, and leverage. The so-called Pareto principle explains the underlying logic as follows:

o In all endeavors, there is invariably an imbalance between inputs and results.

o The majority of inputs have little effect.

- A small minority of inputs make a disproportionate difference to the outputs.
- Identifying and leveraging what the quality guru Joseph Juran called the "vital few" is essential for success.

The Pareto principle is often summarized in what's known as the 80/20 rule, which states that, in most real-world circumstances, 80 percent of the results are driven by 20 percent of the inputs. Here are some examples that illustrate this phenomenon. (The numbers given are approximations, of course; the key point is the mismatch between inputs and results, and the consequent outsized power of leveraging a handful of key inputs.)

- 20 percent of software code drives 80 percent of the usage
- 28 percent of beer drinkers consume 80 percent of the beer
- 15 percent of the world population uses 80 percent of the energy
- 25 percent of the world population owns 80 percent of the wealth

The key takeaway from these varied examples is that there are essentially no decisions that come down to a 50/50 balance of inputs and outputs. To set the right priorities, we need to understand the few things that are most important and focus intensely on those.

Defining Priorities: What Is the Magic Number?

So how many priorities there should be? In my strategy workshops until recently, I emphasized "No more than five priorities." But I've noticed that participants fall prey to the so-called anchoring effect: they seize upon the arbitrary number five and become fixated on naming five priorities. When they get to three or four, they begin to ask themselves the futile question, "What more can we think of?" as they stretch to reach five. In doing so, the whole discipline of focus gets lost, and it becomes a numbers game. Afterwards, few of them can recite all five priorities without a "cheat sheet."

Where does this orthodoxy of five priorities come from? One much-quoted source is a 1956 article by psychologist George Miller called, "The Magic of the Number Seven, Plus or Minus Two." This article purported to show that most people can remember up to seven items in serial-order memory tasks. Take away two, and you are in safe territory with five!

But Nelson Cowan, professor of psychology at the University of Missouri, has identified the flaw in this logic. He points out that, in Miller's experiments, people were able to recall seven items simply because of "chunking" into smaller groupings. For example, a seven-digit phone number is more easily remembered as three chunks: 246-89-21. Remove the chunking or try to remember the number backwards, and you're in trouble. Cowan conducted a study into what he calls *working memory*—the amount of information that can be readily accessible in managing ongoing mental tasks. His research concluded that the human focus of attention is limited. People can follow a maximum of four things, and sometimes fewer.

There is strong evidence to support Cowan's findings.

o   A survey of 1,800 global executives by Paul Leinwand and Cesare Mainardi found that, as an executive team's priority list grows, their company's revenue growth declines relative to its peers. The reverse is also true: they found that organizations with a maximum of three priorities were most likely to achieve above average growth.

o   In an article in the *Sloan Management Review*, Donald Sull, Charles Sull, and James Yoder cite a large survey showing that, in firms with five priorities, only one-quarter of the managers could correctly list three of them.

o   Finally, in a study of 150 hospitals, Wharton professor Drew Carton found that, when hospitals had more than four core values, no improvements were achieved for reducing heart attack readmissions or increasing their return on assets.

The weight of evidence suggests that the degradation of working memory is not linear; it is exponential. Going beyond four priorities risks a wipeout.

So we have good reason to contest the efficacy of setting five priorities. We vastly underestimate the amount of simplification, synthesis, and repetition that is required for employees to buy into even a small set of ideas. A collection of five tends to become a "laundry list" that few can remember, let alone act on.

The Power of Three or Four

Consider the impressive record of the Cleveland Clinic. It was founded in 1921 with a mission to harness integrated medical services in order to excel at three things:

o   Provide better care for the sick
o   Investigate their problems
o   Educate those who serve

The clinic's clear mission and three interrelated priorities add up to a compelling story that has inspired its people, attracted the best talent, and established it as a leader in improving the quality of health care.

Robert Iger offers us another valuable lesson about prioritization. Iger served as the CEO of the Walt Disney Company from 2005 to 2020. During his tenure, the company's market capitalization increased from $48 billion to $257 billion. He tells this story in his book, *The Ride of a Lifetime*: on the lead-up to his appointment, the board asked Iger to define his priorities for the future of the company. He started to make a list, but when he got to five, he realized, "I hadn't prioritized any of them . . . My overall vision lacked clarity and inspiration . . . I quickly landed on three clear priorities. They have guided the company since the moment I was named CEO."

Here, in summary, are the priorities Iger presented to the board:

o We must devote most of our time and capital to the creation of high-quality branded *content*.
o We must embrace *technology* to the fullest extent by using it to create higher quality products and to reach consumers in more modern and relevant ways.

○ We must become a truly *global* company by penetrating certain markets, particularly the world's
most populous countries, like China and India.

Note the stark clarity and memorability of Iger's three
priorities—*content, technology, globalization.* They fit together in an integrated narrative.

So determining the "right" number of priorities is not a
mathematical formula; it is a cognitive challenge based on
the limits of working memory as described by Nelson
Cowan. Three to four priorities appears to be the maximum
number. They work best when we can weave them together
into a compelling story, as Iger and the Cleveland Clinic did.
When we expand the list, we lose the story.

But the Robert Iger example also comes with another
powerful lesson. Nothing lasts forever in a world of constant
change. Iger retired from the CEO role in February 2020.
His successor, Bob Chapek, had to contend with the impacts
of Covid-19 and a series of major changes that roiled the me-
dia industry. Traditional broadcast TV saw steep declines as
customers shifted to the streaming sector, where profits
were being compressed by the effects of intense competition. Disney, with a presence in both traditional TV and
streaming, was caught in a downdraft, and its profitability
and stock price took big hits.

In November 2022, after less than three turbulent years in the role, Chapek was dismissed by the board, which asked Iger to return as CEO.

Disney faced huge choices in terms of overhauling and refocusing its portfolio: what to subtract, what to keep, and what to add.

A year after his return, Iger clarified how the company would concentrate its resources to meet this challenge. The heart of his new vision was to excel at streaming and live experiences. He announced that Disney would pursue this vision by focusing on four building blocks that will provide the springboard for future growth:

- o Upgrade its studios to generate higher quality content
- o Feed this superior content into its streaming business to spur growth and profitability
- o Transform ESPN, its sports network, into a streaming-only business
- o Continue to develop its thriving experiences segment, which includes theme parks and cruises

In a competitive world, there are no guarantees, but Iger has laid the foundations for success by being crystal clear about the things Disney plans to do outstandingly well to restore its fortunes—and by keeping his list of priorities short and tightly focused.

11. Why Focus Wins and Complexity Is Fatal

The difference between successful people
and really successful people is that really
successful people say no to almost everything.

WARREN BUFFETT

A consistent theme that runs through this book is the crucial importance of achieving clarity of focus in all aspects of leadership. My purpose in this chapter is to provide the real-world evidence that demonstrates this imperative and illustrates the dire consequences of ignoring it.

Let's start by reminding ourselves of Carl von Clausewitz's great definition of strategic leadership: "The talent of the strategist is to identify the decisive point and to concentrate everything on it, removing forces from secondary fronts and ignoring lesser objectives." The entire definition is about the primacy of focus.

Here I want to make a crucial point. The wellspring of Clausewitz's formulation is a basic truth that applies in both the military and civilian arenas: every entity, without exception, is confronted with the inescapable reality of limited resources. This is true for all organizations regardless of their size and indeed also for nations. All strategic logic flows from this premise.

This presents us with one of the toughest challenges in leadership. Not only must we concentrate our scarce resources on the right things as Clausewitz stressed; we are forced to contend with a zero-sum process of choice-making whereby every additional thing we do subtracts attention and energy from everything else we do. The inevitable result is that expanding your organization's activities over time without subtraction will debilitate the enterprise.

The simple fact is that complexity is a killer. Two dramatic examples underscore this truth.

The Fall of General Electric

The first example shows the devastating effects of overburdening an organization by striving to do too much. In 2005, General Electric (GE) was the most valuable company in the world. It was widely lauded as the epitome of success—a shining example for others to follow. The company's leaders began to believe that, with good management, GE could do anything. Over time, the company made numerous acquisitions and developed into a sprawling enterprise engaged in the business-to-business, business-to-consumer, and business-to-government sectors, as well as banking. But then, inevitably, it began to pay the price for this complexity. Its lack of focus confused its management and began to undermine its performance. GE lost its way, and the company saw a decline of $500 billion in market value.

GE eventually began to pursue life-saving measures by getting out of its consumer businesses, shrinking its banking business, and concentrating on its industrial businesses. But the change was too little, too late. GE was no longer able to demonstrate that it was more valuable than the sum of its parts, and investors lost confidence in the company.

To save itself, GE is now spinning off its various businesses as independent entities, keeping only its aerospace business as its core activity. GE, in its original conglomerate form, has died. It destroyed itself through the self-inflicted disease of complexity.

The Rise of Apple

Apple, by contrast, illustrates the power of concentration.

The company was founded in 1976 by Steve Jobs and Steve Wozniak, specializing in the development and sale of innovative personal computers. The Apple II was the first commercially successful personal computer. Driven by Jobs' creative flair, the company built on this foundation by selectively adding further high-quality personal digital products and quickly became a profitable, growing enterprise.

However, after losing a boardroom battle, Jobs left Apple in 1985. In the ensuing years, under different CEOs, the company added a large array of products and peripherals with only marginal differences between them. As a result of this clutter and confusion, the company's performance declined precipitously, and by 1996 it was close to collapse.

In 1997, Jobs returned to the company and embarked on a turnaround. In a stunning decision, the first thing he did was reduce Apple's bloated product line by 70 percent, focusing the business on only four key products. Thanks to this intense focus, the turnaround worked brilliantly, and

Apple became the most valuable company in the world, with a market value larger than the entire Russian economy.

Walter Isaacson, Jobs' biographer, reports that Jobs told him, "Deciding what not to do is as important as deciding what to do." Isaacson observed that Jobs "aimed for the simplicity that comes from conquering, rather than merely ignoring, complexity." He relentlessly filtered out what he considered distractions.

Jobs continued to run the company in this vein until his untimely death in October 2011. He took Apple's 100 top executives on retreat each year, and on the last day he would challenge the group to come up with the 10 things the company should do next. Once the group settled on 10, he wrote them on a whiteboard, surveyed them, and systematically deleted seven, declaring, "We can only do three." The whole company would concentrate its resources and creative energies on those three things, with no back burners or side shows permitted. Jobs' leadership approach was totally in tune with Clausewitz's philosophy of concentrating *everything* on the few things that matter most.

The lesson from these contrasting examples is clear: focus energizes and complexity paralyzes. What's needed is a practical leadership discipline to avoid the complexity trap.

Peter Drucker gave us an excellent prescription by advocating that, every three years, every product and activity in an organization should be put on trial for its life. As a former lawyer, I am aware of the rule "innocent until proven guilty." It provides an important safeguard for protecting human rights. However, when it comes to removing underperforming products, the better standard is "guilty until proven innocent."

A pivotal experience of my own entrenched this lesson for me. I vividly recall a difficult decision during my time as president of Seagram USA. Thirty-seven underperforming brands were diverting our focus from our premium brands and dragging down the profits of the overall business, which had declined for four years in a row. There was a clear case to sell these secondary brands and concentrate on the products with greater growth potential and higher profit margins. But how to make the case in the face of resistance? People in the company were personally attached to those brands, and emotions ran high.

I asked Joel, my CFO at the time, to do an analysis of the likely future if we did nothing and allowed current trends to continue. His five-year extrapolation showed that inaction would probably incur many millions of dollars in continuing profit decreases. He then analyzed the alternative future in which the laggard brands would be jettisoned, calculating how fast the higher-margin premium brands would need to grow to overcome the profits forgone by the sale of the laggards. The surprising answer: a mere four percent, a level that everyone agreed was realistic. Based on Joel's comparative analysis, we proceeded to sell the underperforming brands. In the subsequent four years, we comfortably exceeded the four percent growth target, and, without the distraction of the secondary brands, profits surged by 36 percent.

Achieving the goal of focus can be summed up by a simple mantra: *subtract first, then multiply.* This kind of pruning is vital—in fact life-saving—but never easy. Whenever we remove an activity, we are interfering with a love affair; someone in the organization is a champion of that pursuit and cares deeply about it. The leader's task is to explain the broader general interest being served and to take the necessary action with intellectual honesty and compassion.

12. Making Clear-Sighted Decisions in a Confusing World

Leadership is about having the courage to make tough decisions, to take measured risks and to act with integrity.

MARILLYN HEWSON

L eaders are called upon to make numerous decisions every day. Each decision is likely to be challenging in itself—after all, if the right choice was obvious, the problem would likely have been solved before it ever reached the leader's desk. But simply making smart decisions is not enough. To be strategic, the choices you make cannot simply reflect a directionless, scattershot thinking process. The real challenge is to make choices that will systematically guide your organization to a successful future. Like other aspects of leadership, this requires a governing philosophy to give decision-making coherence and consistency.

Here are some decision-making guidelines that have served me well in my own work as a leader, together with lessons I have derived from observing successful leaders in various fields.

First, define the problem you are seeking to solve. If you don't frame a problem in the right way, you will get a poor answer.

For many years, Jacob Jensen was the product designer for Bang & Olufsen's home audio products. He understood the need for a touch of magic in the design to delight the customer. To strengthen his own focus and that of his design team, he avoided vaguely framing his challenge as "designing appealing products." Instead, he sought to create designs that would elicit positive customer reactions to four highly specific questions:

- o Do you want to live with this equipment?
- o Does it make you happy when you see it?
- o When you touch it, can you sense that someone has understood how you communicate with this equipment?
- o Do you smile a little when you discover the heartbeat of the idea?

Because Jensen defined his challenge with such clarity, he was able to produce outstanding creative work, and B & O products are widely admired for both their performance and their beauty.

Design a decision process that reinforces your focus on what matters most.

Once you have framed the problem, don't begin by asking, "What should we do?" Ask first, "What process will we use to make the best decision?" The quality of a decision is heavily dependent on the process you apply.

Here, we come back to Darwinian logic. Remember that your company's survival and success depends on how well it adapts to the challenges posed by a changing environment.

So the best decision-making rule is to apply *outside-in thinking*. Seek first to understand the needs of external stakeholders and the trends in the environment as the basis for your internal actions.

This truth became all too real for me when I was asked to advise an industry study group that had been tasked by regulators to reexamine out-of-date legislation governing industrial policy, then to recommend changes. The way the group had framed the problem seemed sound, but for three months they toiled away, until, in their own words, they "hit a wall." They called me in, hoping I could help them get unstuck.

At our first meeting, the core issue became apparent. Instead of first designing a good decision process, they had simply jumped into a brainstorming mode using the inside-out question, "What should we do?" It was no surprise that this caused them to stall.

We simply redesigned the process with a set of outside-in questions involving an analysis of the interests of the external beneficiaries the industrial policy was designed to serve. In rapid order, the group identified four gaps between what the beneficiaries valued most and what the current policy was offering them. These "value gaps" became the team's solution-building roadmap, making it easy for them to identify a series of specific recommendations for policy improvements.

Their suggestions were unanimously approved by the policy makers. The pivotal factor in their success was simply changing the process by turning the question from inside-out to outside-in.

A good rule of thumb for embedding this principle: "First, look out of the window; then look in the mirror."

Always remember, there is no such thing as a non-decision.

Sometimes you will be tempted to delay or avoid making a tough decision. Taking the time needed to choose wisely is important. But don't forget that delay has its price. The cost of doing nothing is not nothing. Inaction produces its own consequences, and, if you fail to act in a timely fashion, events will make the decision without you.

Therefore, when considering a possible decision, always compare its likely outcome with what would happen if you *don't* take that action. All decisions are comparative: future consequences of inaction must always be weighed against future consequences of the proposed action.

A good example of this is the *sunk cost trap*. Suppose we have embarked on a two-million-dollar project, with payments of one million dollars each due in two phases. We have paid the first million, and the second million is payable unless the project is canceled. When the second payment becomes due, the project is falling short of its targeted return, with little chance of success. What should we do?

In most cases, our instinct is to do nothing and simply allow the additional one million dollars to be paid by default on the theory that we would otherwise have "wasted" the million dollars already invested. But if we pose the question, "What will be the consequences if we *don't* stop the investment?" we get the correct answer: having wasted the first million dollars, we will now also waste the second million! Thus the cost of inaction would far exceed the cost of action.

Challenge the assumptions that drive your decisions.

Peter Drucker claimed that most businesses fail, not because of things done poorly, but because the assumptions on which they were based no longer fit current reality. The problem is that many of our underlying assumptions are silent and implicit; unless we make them explicit and test their validity, they can trip us up.

Here is an example of Drucker's dictum. I've noticed that a frequent but automatic assumption made by business leaders is that their customers place greater importance on product features than on the quality of the customer experience. The evidence shows this is not true—and the flawed assumption drives many unsound business decisions.

During my time as head of Lever Brothers' U.S. Foods Division, I remember reading in an industry publication that an amazingly high percentage of calories in the United States was being consumed in cars. I thought, "That's interesting. I hope they are spreading our margarine on their sandwiches," and casually tossed the magazine away.

The same information was no doubt available to car companies, who similarly ignored it on the assumption that car buyers were mainly motivated by features such as trunk size, seating, performance, and so on. Things didn't change until 1983, when Chrysler responded to the rising in-car consumption of food and beverages by including built-in cupholders for the first time in its new line of minivans. Customers loved the convenience of this benefit and began choosing cars accordingly. Soon all cars were providing cup holders, and manufacturers scrambled to design the best ones and place them in the most accessible locations.

By 2007, PricewaterhouseCoopers was reporting that the number of cup holders was more important to new car buyers than fuel economy. In tune with this finding, the Subaru Ascent now comes with 19 cup holders!

The surprising thing is how long it took for the auto companies to understand what customers valued most—the quality of the driving experience. A key discipline in a changing market is to regularly challenge our underlying assumptions.

Always keep the main thing the main thing.

Coherent decision-making requires relentlessly keeping in mind the main problem we are seeking to solve. The world is a busy, sometimes chaotic place, and we are constantly distracted by onrushing events. To stay focused, we need to maintain a clear frame of reference for our decisions.

The Strategic Learning process described in chapter nine is deliberately designed to provide a practical roadmap for focused decision-making through the entire journey of strategy creation and implementation. When deciding the strategic choices, your main reference point is the challenge you have defined based on the insights from your situation analysis. And when determining your execution program, the main things to keep in the forefront are your winning proposition and your key priorities.

Hans Vestberg, chairman and CEO of Verizon, maintains a steadfast strategic focus with a simple but practical daily discipline. He keeps two lists handy on his desk. On his left is a list of the key priorities of the firm. On his right is his to-do list for operating matters. Every morning, he looks intensely to his left first and reminds himself of the organization's main priorities. Then he looks at the to-do list on the right, picks out the items that would most strongly support these priorities, and tackles those first. This is Vestberg's way of making sure that he never loses sight of the big strategic priorities in the crush of urgent operating matters.

Seek out diverse perspectives, which produce better outcomes than experts working alone.

Research has consistently confirmed this truth. Indeed, I have noticed in my strategy engagements that organizing executives into small, diverse teams to tackle difficult problems often produces breakthrough ideas. Sometimes the solution emerges simply from reframing the problem.

This is what happened in my work with the Girl Scouts of the USA some years ago. The organization's leaders felt they were suffering from a crisis of relevance as membership declined, and they wrestled with defining the benefits they should offer to girls. The programmatic activities such as summer camps and cookie sales were obvious and enduringly popular. But surely these things were a means to an end and not an end in themselves? If so, what was that larger brand promise?

Our first instinct was to gather the marketing and sales experts in a room and ask them to find a solution. But we realized that to generate breakthrough ideas, we needed a different approach. To create a diversity of viewpoints, small cross-functional teams were assigned to labor over the issue. What emerged from this cauldron was the beacon that would light the way forward: *The Girl Scouts' mission is to be the premier leadership experience for girls.* Henceforth, all the organization's energies and programs would be concentrated on bringing this leadership development mission to life.

Don't bet the farm.

Sometimes a very large decision is required in conditions of high uncertainty, and the cost of failure might sink the enterprise—for example, whether to enter a large market like China. Dilemmas of this kind seldom yield a reliable answer through desk analysis alone. The worst thing to do is allow the situation to fester and concede the initiative to competitors. We can't keep our problems on ice and hope to keep them fresh; no learning happens if we just sit still.

Here the best approach is to copy the way science learns: start with a thoughtful hypothesis and then do an experiment, such as a small test market, to see what works and what doesn't. This is a way to adjust the risk/reward ratio: by designing a fast, inexpensive experiment, you create conditions in which the cost of failure is low while the value of the learning is high.

Making Clear-Sighted Decisions in a Confusing World

Accept the reality that you will never have perfect information.

Your decision-making process should not be built around the pursuit of certainty. Leadership is not a safe harbor. In the real world, decisions must be made in conditions of uncertainty. There is always an information deficit between what we know and the decision to be made.

I estimate that in a typical business decision you will probably have access to about 75 percent of the information you would ideally like to know. Yes, it would be nice to increase that ratio—and in life-and-death decisions like rocket science and neurosurgery, doing so is necessary—but even then, there is no 100 percent. Decision-making involves taking prudent risks and managing trade-offs. In most business cases, reliable additional data beyond that 75 percent is simply not available and probably won't improve the quality of your decision. Making a good decision despite the remaining 25 percent gap depends on your judgment, courage and ability to assess the views of others. Ultimately, those are the skills you are paid for.

13. Leading Without Words: The Power of Personal Example

What you do speaks so loudly that I cannot
hear what you say.

RALPH WALDO EMERSON

H umans have the gift of language, which of course is an extraordinarily useful tool for preserving and transmitting knowledge. A talent for using language effectively is a valuable tool in any leader's kit. Yet experience shows that our impact on others derives mainly from the example we set rather than from the words we say or write.

In an earlier chapter, I wrote about the powerful leadership example set by Nelson Mandela. He was an eloquent speaker. Yet most of what the world learned from him was conveyed not by his words, but by his moral courage, dignity, and forbearance. These were the "disturbances" that influenced people everywhere most strongly and helped to change the history of South Africa.

A Lesson from Mandela's Fellow Prisoner

A few years ago, I visited Robben Island off the coast of Cape Town. This is where Mandela was imprisoned prior to his ultimate release and election as South Africa's first Black president. Our guide was a modest, matter-of-fact man who had himself been a prisoner at the same time as Mandela. Our group peppered him with questions, and he gave straightforward, unadorned answers.

"How long were you a prisoner here?"

"Thirteen years."

"Did you suffer a lot?"

"It was very unpleasant."

"Are you angry about what you experienced?"

"There is no point in that. I try to put it behind me."

We could see that were not going to get any histrionics from this man. Finally, I walked out front beside him as he led the group and struck up a more personal conversation.

"I am interested in the idea of forgiveness," I told him. "Usually, we think of forgiveness as a response to a single injustice. But you were subjected to cruelty every day for thirteen years. How on earth did you manage to sustain forgiveness in the face of that repeated onslaught?"

He stopped, looked at me, and said simply, "Mandela was here."

What was life-changing to this man was not what Mandela said. It was what he did.

Mandela, of course, was an icon. But the power of example operates at an everyday level just as it works at the level of national leadership. For instance, as I recounted in chapter one, I often think back on the example of forthrightness and authenticity demonstrated by C.J. van Jaarsveld, my mentor when I was a new CEO.

What My Father Taught Me
About Moral Courage

An even earlier lesson in leadership came from the actions of my father during the global crisis of World War II. My father was not university educated. A down-to-earth man of few words, he was steady and deliberate, with an unflinching moral compass.

There was no conscription in my native South Africa, yet in 1943, with the battle against the Nazis raging across Europe, my father decided to volunteer. It meant leaving his young family to travel far from home in service of a cause that he believed in.

On the day of departure, as my father's train pulled away from the station, beginning his long land and sea journey to the front, I felt pangs of loss and confusion. Tugging at my mother's skirt, I asked, "Why is he going so far away to the war?"

She put an arm on my shoulder and replied, "Because he believes it's the right thing to do."

I didn't realize it at the time, but at the young age of six, I was imbibing one of my first and most important lessons of leadership. Without speaking a word, my father taught me the meaning of moral courage. It is not about seeking danger and adventure for the thrill of it. It is about acting on a core principle and accepting whatever risks are involved.

Fortunately, my father arrived back home safely after the war was won. I've never forgotten the example he set, and I strive to emulate it in the daily challenges of life.

Body Language Can Be Stronger Than Words

The impact of communicating without words played out in an interesting way during my time as a CEO. I had occasion to appoint a new director of financial planning—an important role requiring a high level of analytical rigor. The HR department put forward two outstanding candidates, both women. Let's call them Mary and Isabelle.

During the first interview, both candidates showed they had superb professional qualifications and great experience. I could flip a coin and not go wrong. Afterwards, my assistant, Joanne, asked me what I had decided. "I just don't know," I said. "Both would be excellent in the job. I need more information."

I asked Joanne to arrange a second interview. In that interview, I asked each candidate a question I hadn't used before: "Why do you want this job?"

Both of their verbal responses were good—but the differences in how they expressed them spoke volumes. Mary folded her arms, sat back in her chair, and eloquently expressed her wish to make a meaningful contribution to the department's priorities. When I posed the same question to Isabelle, she voiced sentiments similar to Mary's. But in doing so, she leaned forward eagerly, using her whole body to convey her enthusiasm and commitment. This gesture was totally in tune with what she was saying. That clinched it for me.

After the meetings, Joanne asked me which candidate I'd chosen. "It's Isabelle," I said.

Joanne asked why. "Because she sat forward," I replied.

For a minute, Joanne looked perplexed. Then she smiled as she understood the significance of Isabelle's body language.

The Power of Symbolism

As a leader, I learned that that everything we do carries symbolic impact. An example is deciding what goes on the top of the agenda in meetings. In every speech, a focused leader will emphasize that there is nothing more important than the company's priorities. But a speech is not enough. My golden rule for our monthly progress meetings was always to place the review of those priorities as item one on the agenda. This fortified the message, "There is nothing more important than these." Items at the bottom of an agenda convey a silent message downgrading their importance: "We will get to these if we have time."

It's easy to lose sight of the importance of such nonverbal communication. As leaders, we sometimes forget that everyone is watching. Small gestures can have an outsized effect. Walking into a meeting with a spring in your step and a warm smile can set an upbeat tone that promotes a constructive, can-do approach by the team.

Leaders convey a critical message by the way they react when confronted with bad news. Organizations can learn and improve only if they confront reality and don't bury their mistakes. Of course, it is natural to feel disappointment when presented with bad news. But we underestimate the impact of our nonverbal cues. Gaping with astonishment, rolling our eyes, scowling, shaking our head with disgust—these all project disapproval and perhaps anger, even if we don't say a word. The result is that the messenger feels personally indicted and discouraged from delivering bad news again. "Shooting the messenger" in this way can lead to a breakdown in organizational communication and learning.

Attitude Is Everything

The power of unspoken messages can be wielded by people at every level of an organization. While I was president of Lever Brothers' U.S. foods division, we hired a twenty-one-year-old trainee in our finance department. Steven (as I'll call him) was the embodiment of teamwork and eagerness to help. He was always at the elbow of Art, our CFO, during meetings, offering to tackle problems, follow up on project details, and support others in their work. During long meetings, Steven would sense when the group's energy was flagging and offer to run out and get coffee and bagels for us. He had a boyish smile and soon became immensely popular in the office. Everyone thought of Steven as their friend.

One morning, Art came into my office looking crestfallen. He sat down and gave me the news. Steven had just been diagnosed with terminal brain cancer. He had three months to live.

The sheer tragedy of this awful verdict imposed on this delightful young man pierced me to the core. "Does he know what he's up against?" I asked.

"Yes," said Art. "And he wants to keep working. He loves his job and being part of the team."

Steven kept showing up as usual and throwing himself cheerfully into his work. Aware of his illness, people would ask, "How are you feeling today, Steven?" He would smile and reply, "I'm doing fine, thanks, although the chemo is a bit unpleasant. How are *you*? Did you get that little puppy for your daughter?"

As the days passed, Steven's hair fell out, and he became thinner and weaker, until it was an effort for him to move around. But his smile never waned. We arranged a cab to bring him to the office and take him home every day.

Finally, one morning Steven didn't show up. A cloud of gloom hung over the office as we processed the inevitable reality. Two days later, we learned that he was gone.

Steven's lessons about life have stayed with me and, I suspect, with everyone in that office. His motto: "No complaints." His unspoken message: "I'm only here for a short time. What can I do for you?"

14. Lessons from Maisie: What I Learned About Leadership from My Dog

It is amazing how much love and laughter dogs bring into our lives and how much closer we become to each other because of them.

JOHN GROGAN

I t might seem strange to include a chapter about a dog in a book on leadership, but I do so for an important reason. One of my most surprising and rewarding learning experiences came from my relationship with a black Lab called Maisie.

Dogs touch aspects of our personalities that others seldom see, and that we ourselves often neglect or even suppress. They connect with our playful selves, our emotional selves, our nonverbal selves, our intuitive selves. The dogs who join our households can share their lives with us more deeply and completely than even our family members do, making their personalities felt through all five senses (including smell!) and imprinting their presence on every moment of our days. In the process, they teach us to become fully ourselves—and fully human.

Maisie came to us from the Guiding Eyes for the Blind, which trains dogs to serve as companions and helpers for people with visual impairment. At 18 months, she had "failed" her final test, thus becoming what they euphemistically call a "release dog" and made available for adoption. Having heard good things about the dogs raised by Guiding Eyes, my wife, Laura, and I applied for an adoption, and in due course we were approved to become Maisie's new family. We excitedly welcomed her into our home.

Certain memories become embedded in our minds. So it was the day Maisie joined our family. I saw her for the first time when I got home from a day of teaching. We looked intently at each other, in a kind of mutual sizing-up. She was a sleek, beautifully athletic youngster, exuding curiosity and eagerness. After a brief inspection, her tail began to wag, and she trotted towards me for our first greeting. She had decided I was okay. What struck me most that day were Maisie's deep brown eyes; shining and youthful, but somehow also discerning and wise.

It soon became apparent why Maisie had failed to clear the final hurdle at Guiding Eyes for the Blind—she was just too eager to please, energetic, and curious. She would likely have led a blind person into all kinds of playful but inadvisable adventures. As a therapy dog, Maisie would have been misplaced—but for my wife and me, she was an ideal companion.

From then on, Maisie and I walked the path of life together. We developed a growing bond built on time spent together in my home office, daily walks in the park, playing chase, often traveling together. We were seldom apart, and we learned to understand each other's moods, needs, and expectations.

It is a truism that we are closest to those who have been our lifelong friends. Maisie knew me for a fourteen-year slice of my life, but I knew her through all her life stages—from her exuberant squirrel-chasing youth, through her more sedate middle age, to her faltering old age and eventual demise. Despite this mismatch in our life cycles, I would venture that Maisie knew me at least as well as I knew her, and in a number of respects even better.

It was this human-canine relationship that revealed to me some of my most important lessons about life and leadership.

The Real Meaning of Transparency

In the business world, we emphasize how important it is for companies and their leaders to be "transparent." To clarify this buzzword, we come up with sophisticated definitions of what this means, from the rules of full disclosure in financial statements to simple calls for honesty in our dealings with others.

When this topic comes up in my seminars, I reflect on what I learned from Maisie and sometimes ask how many attendees own a dog. Usually the number is around 50 percent. To them I offer this advice, "If you want to understand what true transparency looks like, observe your dog." I then ask the dog owners to describe to the rest of the group what they see in their dog's behavior. What follows is a great discussion about the real meaning of transparency.

Day in and day out, Maisie revealed her mood or feelings without reservation, whether she was feeling joy, fear, pain, hunger, playfulness, or just the need for a walk. No pretenses, no vanity, no ulterior motives, no fear of being judged; just plain honesty and most important of all, humility. I can't think of a better transparency checklist for business leaders.

The Power of Encouragement

Maisie loved to learn new things, and I sometimes worked with a dog trainer to add to her repertoire. At a certain point the trainer said, "You are Maisie's mentor, so you should take over the training now. It's part of your relationship with her."

Feeling unprepared, I sought further advice. "What is the key to training a dog well? Repetition, discipline, lots of rewards?"

The trainer replied, "Yes, all those. But you have left out the biggest one—*encouragement*. Give her a sense of achievement by setting manageable tasks; praise her when she succeeds; restore her confidence when she fails and help her try again; never let her lose her dignity."

That lesson in dog training hit home for me. My attitude up to that point had been rather shallow, thinking that as a dog Maisie could only learn by rote—that belief in herself didn't matter. I had forgotten the most important task of a leader: to help others overcome self-doubt and realize their best selves. It was a revelation to see what a difference encouraging the spirit makes, as much in the canine species as in the human one.

The Importance of Enthusiasm

I don't think there is a more consequential leadership attribute than enthusiasm. It literally changes our chemistry, drives us forward, helps us overcome hurdles, and inspires cooperation in others. The magic of enthusiasm is that it is infectious. When a leader is fired with energy and excitement about a new project, others in the organization are likely to catch the bug.

My daily dose of enthusiasm came from Maisie. She responded with the same zest and joy to both small and big things, from a car ride or a new toy to a visit from a friend. During our early morning walks in Central Park, she sniffed the air with expectation, played eagerly with other dogs, chased the ball with a joyful vigor, and licked the hands of her favorite people. Seeing her in full flight was a wondrous, uplifting sight. Whatever she was doing, she was all in, fully committed.

When I would get back to my office after our walk to start the workday, with Maisie resting at my feet, I was infused with positive energy. Everything felt brighter and more hopeful. Life was good.

Notice To Visitors

1. The dog lives here. You don't.
2. If you don't want the dog to be near you, stay off the furniture.
3. Yes, she has some disgusting habits. So do I and so do you. What's your point?
4. OF COURSE she smells like a dog.
5. It's her nature to try to sniff your crotch. Please feel free to sniff hers.
6. I like her a lot better than I like most people.
7. To you she's a dog. To me she's an adopted daughter who is short, hairy, walks on all fours and doesn't speak clearly. I have no problem with any of these things.

Figure 14.1. Notice to Visitors Concerning Maisie

A touch of humor can brighten the mood. One day, I found a whimsical notice on the internet, posted by an anonymous source. I printed and framed it and placed it in my office in a location where visitors could see it (Figure 14-1). Invariably, we started our meetings with a smile.

The Magic of Empathy

Maisie mastered an impressive array of commands, and she enjoyed learning new ones. However, most of our communication was nonverbal. Any dog owner will recognize the behavior of a dog upon seeing a suitcase being packed: tail between the legs, head bowed, shadowing the owner around the house. The disappointment is clearly expressed: "Please don't leave me."

As I was a regular traveler, this was a common occurrence. So, to spare Maisie from distress, I decided on a plot to conceal my travel. No packing, no suitcase, no visible signs of travel until the last minute. But something interesting happened. Without any concrete evidence, Maisie sensed my impending departure and showed her disappointment. What was it? Did she pick up key words like "passport" or "tickets," or was it a subtle change in my nervous energy or scent? I never figured out what triggered it, but one way or another, Maisie got the message at an intuitive level. She was simply much better at interpreting me than I was her.

Empathy means seeing the world through the eyes of others. The best leaders recognize the importance of this kind of understanding, and that the key to this is the ability to listen well. But words are inefficient, and humans often use them to shield their real feelings. Maisie reminded me that the highest art of listening is the ability to hear what is not being said, but nevertheless being felt.

Living in the Moment

The Roman philosopher and statesman Seneca counseled that "The greatest obstacle to living is expectancy, which hangs upon tomorrow and loses today." The Russian novelist Tolstoy reminded us that today is the only time when we have power to act. We readily acknowledge the wisdom of these insights—yet how hard it is for us humans to live in the here and now. We pride ourselves on our ability to interpret the past and contemplate the future, and in the process we forsake the present.

It is always instructive to hear the stories of people who have been through a near-death event. It often jolts them into experiencing the rest of their lives in the present tense, and they tell us how transformative this has been.

In this regard, animals are wiser than we are. Being with Maisie was a daily reminder of what it means to live in the moment, to experience life as it unfolds. If I could have asked her, "Maisie, what time is it?" she would have answered, "The time is now." Ah, yes, of course it is . . .

The Meaning of Trust

My time with Maisie helped me think of trust in new ways. In important respects, we depended on each other and enriched each other's lives. But clearly, she was the more vulnerable partner—to mistreatment or neglect, for example. I realized that the ultimate test of trust is how we treat those who rely on us but have no means of retaliation when we fail them. The abuse of power is the biggest breach of all.

All this came into sharp and wrenching focus when Maisie reached the final stages of her life. Old age began to ravage her, and she struggled more and more. Under the watchful eye of our vet, we made sure she wasn't suffering pain, and kept putting off the awful moment when it would be time to let her go. We wanted to hold on to her as long as possible. But her discomfort and distress increased, and her joy of life faded away. We knew the end was coming soon, but we needed a signal.

On a sunny April day, I took Maisie out for a gentle walk. At a certain point, she stumbled and glanced up at me. Those wise brown eyes conveyed a message, "I think it's time." Maisie trusted me to understand when her time was up, and to be with her when the end came. The vet was kind and understanding. Tears were okay as Laura and I said farewell to our treasured friend.

As the years have passed, my wife and I still smile when we recall some of Maisie's more colorful escapades. She was, to put it mildly, food obsessed and a relentless forager. She was an expert at using her playfulness and guile to make her "hits."

One day while walking her in the park, I came across a family with a small child about two years of age. The little girl was eating an ice cream. She saw Maisie and was keen to pet her. The family was delighted and took photos while this was going on. Meanwhile, the ice cream was melting, and Maisie softly licked the trickles running down the cone and onto the child's hand. The child chortled with delight.

Finally, having charmed everyone, Maisie very gently gulped down the entire ice cream, leaving an empty cone. Rather than being upset, the child and her parents laughed joyfully. "Thank you so much for letting our daughter play with your dog," said the parents as Maisie and I continued on our way.

If life's disturbances are the chief triggers of learning, sometimes the most impactful disturbances can be ones that provoke smiles and laughter along the way.

15. Building Trust: The Touchstone of Leadership

Trust has no gradient.

TOBA BETA

I n the previous chapter, I wrote about the vital role of trust in sustaining our relationships with our canine companions. The same applies to sustaining successful leadership of humans. When trust is violated, leadership is undermined. This is true not only for individual leaders, but also for brands and companies. Which raises the big question, How can we actually build, measure, and sustain trust? What specific attitudes and behaviors are required?

Some years ago, a client of mine in the professional services business announced the goal of making their firm a "trusted advisor" to its clients. This was a worthy ambition—but what exactly did it mean? The firm hired me to help them by defining the essential building blocks of trust—a stepping stone to the creation of a client service model they could use when training their executives, as well as a measurement system they could apply to assess their effectiveness.

I was grateful for the opportunity to learn about trust. Based on my inquiry, I came up with the following components that I believe can serve as a guide to trust-based leadership in any setting. Employees, customers, and investors will trust you if you consistently demonstrate these five things.

You understand their needs.

One of our most deeply felt human needs is the desire to be fully understood. When understanding is missing from any relationship, loss of trust and rejection are likely to result.

Genuine understanding requires empathy. This demands one of the rarest of all skills—the ability to genuinely listen to another person, suspending judgment and simply listening to understand. When we listen deeply, we convey that we value the person we are listening to.

Perhaps you've heard the joke about the patient who walks into a doctor's office and is immediately greeted with the words, "I've already prepared your prescription!" When the surprised patient replies, "But you haven't heard my complaint yet!" the doctor responds, "Yes, but this worked for my last patient, so I'm assuming it will work for you." It's safe to say that this doctor is not a very good listener—and that he is unlikely to win the trust of his patient.

Research by Dr. Heidi Halvorson at Columbia Business School shows that the initial decision to trust is made subconsciously and is based to a large extent on how a person projects warmth and takes the time to understand what is being said to him. If you want to be considered trustworthy, Dr. Halvorson advises, "Take the time to mentally put yourself in your interlocutor's shoes, to really try to grasp their perspective. Use phrases like 'I imagine you must feel' to convey that empathy directly."

Of course, what really matters is not simply the *appearance* of empathy; it's the *demonstration* of empathy. This is exhibited when we close the loop from a passive understanding of what is being conveyed to acting on it. Which leads us to the second building block of trust.

You have the skills to solve their problem.

If we are going to trust someone to serve our needs, it is important that they demonstrate both understanding of those needs and the competence required to address them. For example, we expect our tax accountant to prepare our return legally and efficiently, our cable technician to restore our service, and our auto mechanic to get our car functioning again. If they fail, so will our trust in them, and we will give future jobs to someone else.

Equally important is *social* competence. If a provider does a good job but with a poor attitude, it undermines the total customer experience. Customers place a high value on elements of social behavior like promptness, courtesy, and a readiness to answer questions honestly. If social competence is missing, even if technical competence is present, my trust will be impaired, and I probably will begin to look for solutions elsewhere.

You care about their success.

Trust means having someone else's best interests at heart. It is compromised if we feel that someone is acting with selfish motives or a hidden agenda. Sadly, our politicians today often appear to take positions aimed primarily at keeping themselves in power while pretending to serve the interests of voters. As a result, the public approval rating for the U.S. Congress is at an all-time low. No personal relationship could survive at such low levels of trust.

It is often the small gestures of caring rather than the grand declarations that matter most. I shop regularly at the Publix supermarket during my winter sojourns in Florida. Whenever I inquire about the location of an item, the floor worker will cheerfully lead me there rather than just pointing at or reciting the aisle number. A little thing, but it reinforces the sense that the employees care about the needs of customers and demonstrate that caring through concrete behaviors.

And of course, going the extra mile speaks volumes. The most valuable gift you can give to others is your time. This is true in both professional relationships and personal ones.

You keep your promises.

Consistency is a crucial aspect of trust. It is about keeping promises large and small.

The importance of promise-keeping applies not just in personal relationships but also at a corporate level. Brands, for example, are based on promises to customers, and a brand's destiny in the marketplace depends on the degree to which it keeps that underlying promise.

The famous story of the 1982 Tylenol crisis illustrates this truth vividly. When seven people in the Chicago area died after purchasing capsules of Extra-Strength Tylenol that had been laced with cyanide, Johnson & Johnson, which owned the Tylenol brand, accepted full responsibility. Although the problem was apparently confined to the Chicago area, the company issued a nationwide recall of all Tylenol products, with a retail value of almost $300 million in today's money. It did not reintroduce the brand until it had researched and pioneered the use of tamper-resistant packaging. Through its actions, J&J sent this message to the public: "We will keep our promise to protect your safety above all else, regardless of the cost to us."

During the crisis, Tylenol's market share collapsed from thirty-five percent to eight percent. But it had retained the trust of its customers, and within several years, the brand had regained its status as the leading over-the-counter pain medicine in the United States.

You are a truth teller.

Telling the occasional "white lie" is a social grace when it is done to protect another's self-esteem ("The dinner was fine, I'm just not very hungry this evening"). This is commonly understood. But we cross a line when we knowingly tell a lie or disguise the truth in a way that places another at a disadvantage.

Bobby Jones was a famous golfer with an outstanding record. In the 1925 U.S. Open, he was preparing to hit a shot out of the rough at a critical moment. As he readied himself, he felt his club accidentally touch the ball and move it a tiny fraction of an inch. He gained absolutely no advantage, and no one else saw him touch the ball, but Jones called a one-stroke penalty on himself. He went on to lose the championship—by one stroke. When fans praised his selfless action, Jones dismissed their accolades by saying, "You might as well praise me for not robbing a bank."

Jones's high standard of truthfulness exemplified the behavior of a person who consistently earns, and keeps, the trust of others.

In times of crisis, truth-telling can be especially hard—but crucial. When I was named president of Lever Brothers' Foods Division in the United States, the company was losing a lot of money in its margarine business. We had to take the painful step of closing our margarine plant in a gritty neighborhood of Hammond, Indiana, which would require a six-month transition.

I was warned that closing our plant there was going to be difficult. There was much debate at company headquarters in New York over how to handle the closing. "Don't tell the workers anything until four weeks before we close the plant," some advised. "It's a rough crowd out there. If we tell them now, they'll be furious, our efficiencies will drop through the floor, and our losses will get even worse."

These arguments ignored a key point: that if the workers heard about the closing from anyone other than their leaders—which was likely—distorted rumors would probably spread, causing trust and morale to plummet. I flew out to Hammond to deliver the news promptly, accompanied by our head of operations.

When some 350 workers were assembled, I stood up and told them that I was there to speak as honestly as I could about the state of the business. "We need to close this plant in six months' time," I said. I admitted that I was nervous and hated telling them this, and that I wished it were otherwise. "But," I said, "We can't see any other way of saving the company." I promised a bonus to everyone if they kept productivity at current levels.

To my surprise, there was applause after I had finished. I turned to our head of operations and said, "What is going on? This is the first time I've ever heard people applauding the news that they're out of a job!"

"I think they're applauding our honesty," he replied.

An even bigger surprise was to follow. I was afraid that, despite the bonuses, productivity at the plant would drop along with morale, which could potentially cost us millions of dollars. But in the next six months, productivity at Hammond actually *increased* to its highest levels in five years. On one of my subsequent visits to the plant, I asked a union leader to explain the reason for this. He raised his chin, and answered with one word: "Pride."

It was a defining moment for me.

16. To Lead Is to Teach: The Power of Storytelling

The Universe is made of stories, not of atoms.

MURIEL RUKEYSER

I n prior chapters, I've emphasized the need for organizations to clarify their winning proposition and their key priorities for success. However, if those ideas reside only within the executive suite or are buried in complex documents, employees cannot be energized by them. To quote former secretary of state Henry Kissinger, "No foreign policy—no matter how ingenious—has any chance of succeeding if it is born in the minds of a few and carried in the hearts of none." The same applies to business strategy.

How can leaders ensure that their strategic mission is carried in both the minds and hearts of all their employees?

Many companies try to address this challenge through purely analytical arguments. They present dozens of dense PowerPoint slides at a town hall meeting and then expect employees to understand the logic and gallop off enthusiastically and do everything it takes to implement the strategy. This approach is likely to fail. Employees are not motivated by PowerPoints. They are inspired by leaders and ideas.

To move people at the deepest level, we need to communicate ideas through compelling stories. In an interview in *Strategy + Business*, developmental psychologist Howard Gardner emphasized the importance of storytelling to engage and motivate employees. "People have a real thirst for stories that give them a better sense of how they belong," he said. He emphasized that effective leadership involves the creation of powerful narratives, and that the greater the change you aim to make, the more important the story becomes.

In other words, leaders need to return to one of our oldest human traditions, that of storytelling.

The evidence supports Gardner's view that employee engagement has a direct impact on success. A Gallup Survey found that companies in the top quartile of employee engagement achieved 22 percent higher profits than those in the bottom quartile.

3M has embraced this concept by transforming the business plan from a list of bullet points into a narrative that tells everyone what the strategic goals are, explains the logic behind those goals, and defines what's required to reach them.

So storytelling is a crucial skill for leaders to master. But, like any other skill, it does not come naturally to all leaders and needs to be purposefully developed. Must one be an extrovert to be good at telling stories? I don't think so. Some of the best storytellers I've witnessed have been introverts. I believe it's a matter of authenticity, empathy, and imagination.

What are the ingredients of effective stories? I suggest they contain the following essentials.

They simplify complexity.

Simplification is attention-getting. To focus their organizations on the few things that matter most, leaders must be able to create simplicity in a world of increasing complexity. But simplicity is hard work. First, it is necessary to cut through the clutter and identify the core of an issue. Then this core idea must be conveyed with a compelling story that ensures everyone's attention is focused on this singular issue.

Let's turn to the Gettysburg Address as an example. This speech, perhaps the most famous in American history, was given by Abraham Lincoln in November 1863 at a ceremony overlooking the scene of the epic and bloody Civil War battle of Gettysburg. The purpose of the event was to dedicate the Soldiers' National Cemetery and, in the process, to vindicate the cause for which so many Union soldiers had given their lives.

The main speaker at the event was Edward Everett. An eminent man, he had been president of Harvard, a U.S. senator, and a secretary of state. He spoke for two hours and used 13,500 words. Nobody remembers what he said.

Abraham Lincoln followed and spoke for three minutes, using 280 words, and it is Lincoln's simple message with its vivid imagery that is remembered as the Gettysburg Address. His powerful theme of protecting the principles of a democratic republic has been recalled and quoted repeatedly for the past 160 years.

They engage people emotionally through vivid metaphors, examples, and pictures.

Cold logic has a limited impact. Commitment and motivation involve our feelings. The magic lies in the illustrative use of symbols and examples. As an educator, I notice that whenever I say, "Let me give you an example" or "Here's a picture of what I mean," everyone sits up in anticipation of learning something. The power of a metaphor is that it is open-ended, leaving room in the minds of listeners to do some creative translation of their own. This engenders a personal investment in the idea.

One example hearkens back to my origins in South Africa. At my uncle's farm where I often spent school holidays (as recalled in chapter six), it was a tribal custom for the children to help by collecting dry wood at sunset for cooking meals and keeping their family huts warm at night. The kids took pride in the number of dry sticks they could gather.

As the story goes, a tribal elder used this practice as an opportunity to illustrate the virtue that "unity builds strength." When a 10-year-old came running back enthusiastically with his bundle of dry sticks, the elder praised him and said, "Put them down on the ground." Then he asked the boy to pick up one stick and break it, which the youngster easily did.

"Well done!" said the elder. "Now pick up three sticks and break them."

After struggling for a while, the boy gave up and said, "I can't do it. I'm only ten. You do it."

While the boy watched, the elder tried to break the three sticks but also found it impossible. "You see," he said, "sticks in a bundle are unbreakable."

Far more memorable than a tedious lecture about unity, this simple illustration and its symbolism provided a lifetime lesson for the young boy.

I told this story to the executives at the Girl Scouts of the USA during my work helping them to build a cohesive culture. The metaphor took hold, and they began placing neatly tied bundles of sticks in all their conference rooms at their Edith May training center as a silent but powerful reminder of the importance of unity and teamwork.

They raise—and resolve—important issues.

Stories are provocative. There is suspense involved when a question is framed, and the answer is not yet clear. Then comes the resolution and the "Aha" moment. The experiences such stories lead us through become lodged in our memory bank.

Here's an example from the work of philosopher John Rawls. He observes that young people often struggle to define the values that will shape their lives—their command center, if you like. He then offers a brilliant metaphor to help anyone fulfill that crucial task, based on the simple learning device of "the veil of secrecy." Imagine that you are not yet born but have been provided with the miraculous gift of deciding what kind of world you will be born into. Now here's the catch: you don't know whether you will be born male or female, healthy or sickly, white or brown, rich or poor. A veil of secrecy hides all these details from you. With this proviso, write down a description of the kind of world you'd want to live in.

The image of the veil of secrecy forces us to take a fair and impartial view of social, political, and economic arrangements, untainted by any self-interest. It makes us think hard about how to create a society where all people have an equal chance at happiness, regardless of their circumstances. It's a great example of how story-based imagery can stimulate our thinking and open our minds.

They sound a call to action.

The best leaders use stories to influence the thoughts, feelings, and behaviors of those they seek to lead. Their ultimate purpose is to guide behavior—but commitment to an idea must come first.

Ex-president Bill Clinton relates how he became frustrated with point-scoring and turf battles during policy meetings in the Oval Office. Pleading and cajoling didn't help.

Then he had an idea. He borrowed a moon rock from NASA and placed it on the table in the center of the room. "For the next two years," he recalls, "when we'd have people on two sides of any issue, and they'd start getting out of control, I'd say, Wait! You see that moon rock? It's 3.6 billion years old. We're just passing through here and we don't have very much time, so let's calm down and figure out the right thing to do." He added, "It worked every single time." Clinton's adroit use of symbolism played an important role in getting adversaries to see a broader perspective and collaborate more effectively.

They are embodied by their messengers.

The key to persuasion is authenticity. An audience senses a fake in minutes—sometimes in seconds. To be effective, a story must represent the sincere convictions of the leader and be exemplified consistently by his or her own behavior.

In chapter two, I described the way Nelson Mandela was able to transform South Africa from a country riven by racial injustice into an inclusive democracy. In service of his vision of a Rainbow Nation, he exhorted forgiveness and reconciliation. But he didn't just preach this message. He lived it every day, both in big, sweeping actions and in small, personal gestures. Otherwise, his words would have been hollow and would have failed to persuade.

Stories make meaning. They respond to our universal search for causes and effects, for a sense of purpose and belonging. At their best, they help to unite people behind a shared narrative and a common purpose. Then, as the legendary senator Daniel Webster said, "People can do jointly what they cannot do singly. The union of minds and hands, the concentration of their power, becomes almost omnipotent."

The challenges we face in running organizations continue to evolve. So do the means of communication at our disposal. Since the onset of Covid-19, we have embarked on a giant set of experiments on how best to manage hybrid home/office work. This learning has been abetted by the arrival of more effective online conferencing tools. But these remote ways of working often fail to produce the same feelings of attachment as in-person interactions. There are difficult trade-offs to be resolved, and we don't yet know how this will settle out.

But one thing is clear: in the new world of work, the bonding power of storytelling will become a more crucial part of a leader's repertoire than ever.

Epilogue:
The World Is a Gift of Learning

We are born to be a witness to the mystery of the universe
and to discover who we are, where we fit in,
and how to live our lives.

ADAPTED FROM RAY BRADBURY

A s I conclude this exploration of leadership, I return to the central theme of this book. Leadership is a philosophy as much as anything else—an integrated set of ideas and principles that represent a leader's command center and serve as both a guide and a spur to action. I hope these pages have shown that this philosophy boils down to mobilizing the effective combination of character and competence. Both are important, but it is character that gives leadership its humanity, its purpose, and its meaning. Competence can be delegated or purchased. Character must be self-made, and we alone own it.

The Features of Character and Competence

To help us think more intentionally about building our leadership character and competence, let's clarify the defining features of each aspect. My view of these is shown in the Leadership Cube (Figure E-1).*

---

* This model echoes the U.S. Army's *Be, Know, Do* unified theory of leadership as outlined in its Field Manual number 22-100, so I am using the same headings here.

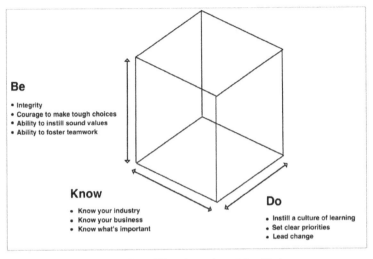

Be
- Integrity
- Courage to make tough choices
- Ability to instill sound values
- Ability to foster teamwork

Know
- Know your industry
- Know your business
- Know what's important

Do
- Instill a culture of learning
- Set clear priorities
- Lead change

Figure E.1. The Leadership Cube

o *Be* represents a leader's character—the internal qualities that define who you are and embody the foundations of your leadership.

o *Know* is about possessing the basic competencies to lead effectively.

o *Do* is about leveraging character and competence to do what is necessary to address the specific circumstances you face.

This formula makes more explicit the factors that help us to become integrated leaders as described in chapter one. I have found it an enormously useful framework for thinking about the underlying philosophy that comprises my own command center.

In the same way that these ideas have inspired me, I hope that they will help you think about how you will cultivate your own garden. The word *philosophy* comes from the Greek *philosophia*, meaning "the love of wisdom." Authentic leaders are seekers of wisdom in a constant quest to help them better meet the challenges they face.

As each of us follows our own pathway, we would do well to remember the wisdom of Margaret Wheatley's dictum: "You cannot change a living thing from the outside. You can only disturb it, so it changes itself." Leadership is not conferred by formal appointment to a position of authority. Instead, it is deliberately self-generated, sparked by the ways in which we develop and grow in response to the disturbances we experience in the course of life. Our task is to search for the stimuli that will light the way—the more diverse, the better.

Here we come full circle to a key message in this book. Leadership and learning are inseparable parts of each other. Leadership, then, is an unending journey. We all have certain innate attributes—our genetic baseline, if you like. But this is simply an inherited starting point. Our most important endowment is the capacity to learn and grow. Imbuing an organization with this capacity is a leader's most important responsibility.

Epilogue

As Charles Darwin has taught us, the ultimate survivors in a changing world will be the best learners.

Acknowledgments

Bringing this book to fruition has reinforced my understanding that we achieve nothing of consequence on our own. Many others contribute to our life's endeavors and deserve our gratitude for doing so.

A big vote of thanks goes to my wife, Laura, who encouraged me to write this book in the first place. An accomplished author in her own right, she has been my unflagging cheerleader and generous sounding board along the way. Her insights have been invaluable.

To Karl Weber, my editor and founder of Rivertowns Books, my warm thanks for his professionalism and grace and for teaching me that books need to have "room to breathe." Karl brought his extensive experience, creativity, and generosity of spirit to this project.

I want to thank my colleagues and good friends at Columbia Business School for the rich exchange of ideas that have inspired me to do my best thinking. My time at the School has been an exercise in continuing education.

Finally, my thanks to my loyal assistant and supportive colleague for the past twenty years, Aimee Chu, whose belief is that her job description imposes no boundaries. Aimee diligently and cheerfully manages the daily office affairs, ensuring as she does so that I have the space to concentrate on my teaching, consulting, and writing. That is a contribution far greater than she realizes.

W.P.

New York City

September, 2024

Index

Index

automotive industry, change in, 49–50, 143
awareness
  of bias, 57
  learning and, 38–39

bad news, reactions to, 155
Bang & Olufsen (B & O), 138
Be aspect, of Leadership Cube and, 193
Beethoven, Ludwig van, 88
behavior
  care and, 174–75
  learning and, 38, 42–44, 69, 79
  negative, 23, 97–98
  stories and, 187–88
Benn, Tony, 65, 66
bias, 55–56
  awareness of, 57
  confirmation, 49–50
  denial and, 52–54
  objectivity and, 48–49
  status quo, 51–52
  unlearning and, 79–80
Blackberry, 104–5
blind spots, 98, 102
B & O. *See* Bang & Olufsen
body language, 153–54
Boeing, 99–100
Bonaparte, Napoleon, 118
bosses, subordinates and, 97, 99–102. *See also* leaders
bottom-up information, 96–102
brand promise, 145, 176
business environments
  challenges and, 92–93
  pace of, 88–89, 114–15

CALL. *See* Center for Army Lessons Learned
care, 135
  behavior and, 174–75
Center for Army Lessons Learned (CALL), 70–71, 112

CEOs, intimidation and, 97–98
challenges, 12, 92–93
  change and, 125–26
  confirmation bias and, 49–50
  definition of, 144
  denial and, 53–54
  design and, 138–39
  disruption and, 89
  leading up as, 97, 100
  Mandela and, 24–27
  questions and, 64
  South Africa and, 32–33
change
  in automotive industry, 49–50, 143
  challenges and, 125–26
  climate, 53–54
  collective ownership of, 30–31
  digital age and, 12, 37, 51–52, 105–6, 132
  environmental, 51
  pace of business and, 114–15
  political, 22–34
  profits and, 49–50, 99–100, 125–26, 134–35
  renewal and, 108
  strategy and, 104–6, 112
Chapek, Bob, 125–26
character, 34
  Be aspect and, 193
  competence and, 11–12, 18–19, 192–94
  of Mandela, 26
Chobani, 113–14
choices
  of customers, 111
  resources and, 130
  success and, 138
Chrysler, 143
Civil War, U.S., 184–85
clarity
  creativity and, 133, 139
  decisions and, 138–47
  of focus, 130

learning and, 39–41
priorities and, 31–32, 123–27, 182, 194
questions and, 72
Clausewitz, Carl von, 114, 130
    On War, 118–19
Clear, James, *Atomic Habits*, 38
Cleveland Clinic, 123–24
climate change, denial and, 53–54
Clinton, Bill, 188
collective ownership, of change, 30–31
Columbia Business School, 41, 114, 173
command center, of leaders, 10, 46, 96, 187, 192, 194
commodity, customers and, 112–13
communication, 96, 182, 189
    discussion and, 29, 45, 57, 60, 63–64, 82, 100–101
    nonverbal, 153–55, 165–66, 168
    organizational, 155
competence, 40
    character and, 11–12, 18–19, 192–94
    Know aspect and, 194
    operations and, 19
    understanding and, 174
competition, 195
    learning and, 36–37
    priorities and, 126–27
    Strategic Learning and, 112–13
competitive advantage, 16, 107
    disruption and, 106
    Focus step and, 110
    ideas and, 119
    strategy and, 104
complexity
    critical thinking and, 48
    failure and, 131–32
    focus and, 130–35, 184
    insight and, 93
concentration, 119
    success and, 132–33

confirmation bias, 49–50
connections, 86, 160
    insight and, 89–90
consequences, of inaction, 53, 99–100, 141–42
consistency, 138
    trust and, 176–77
context, 10–11
    thought and, 89–90
Cook, Tim, 10
cooperation, 37, 56–57, 188
    enthusiasm and, 164
cost/benefit analysis, 54
costs
    failure, 146
    strategy and, 50
    sunk, 141–42
courage, 102, 147
    moral, 150, 152–53
Covid-19 pandemic, 71–72, 125, 189
Cowan, Nelson, 122, 125
creativity, 42
    clarity and, 133, 139
    walks and, 86–93
crisis, 50, 176
    honesty and, 177–79
critical thinking, 48–49
cultivation, of garden, 10–11, 14, 192.
        See also personal philosophy
culture, of organizations, 44–46, 98, 100–101, 108, 194
curiosity, 46, 77, 161
    learning and, 41–42
curse, of power, 97–100
customer experience, 56, 69–70, 142–43, 174
customers, 55–56, 68
    choices of, 111
    commodity and, 112–13
    disruption and, 113–14
    empathy and, 70
    employees and, 69–70
    reactions of, 138–39
    success and, 67

Index

Index

Index

Miller, George, 121–22
mission, of organizations
    analysis and, 182
    diverse perspectives and, 145–46
    employees and, 69
    value and, 111–12
moral courage, 150, 152–53
morale, trust and, 178
motivation, 194
    Align step and, 108
    stories and, 182–83

narratives, purpose and, 124–25,
    182–83, 189
natural world, humanity and, 86, 160
Neanderthals, *Homo sapiens and,*
    36–37
needs
    human, 113, 189
    of stakeholders, 18, 55–56, 140,
      175
    understanding of, 173–74
negative behavior, 23, 97–98
new ideas, feedback and, 96–97
new knowledge, 44
new technology, 104–6
Nietzsche, Friedrich, 88
Nokia, 104–5
nonverbal communication, 155
    body language as, 153–54
    Maisie and, 165–66
    trust and, 168

Obama, Barack, 104
objectivity, 57
    bias and, 48–49
Ogilvy, David, 101–2
On War (Clausewitz), 118–19
Open AI, 105–6
openness
    critical thinking and, 49
    hierarchies and, 100–101
    improvement and, 101–2
operations

intelligence and, 109
people compared to, 17–19
organizations
    adaptation and, 12–13, 107
    communication in, 155
    culture of, 44–46, 98, 100–101,
      108, 194
    mission of, 69, 111–12, 145–46,
      182
    services of, 56, 112–13, 123–24
    social contract of, 100–101
    sustainability of, 106, 114–15
    trust in, 172
outside-in process, 110
    decisions and, 140–41

pace, of business environments
    change and, 114–15
    thinking tools and, 88–89
Palmisano, Sam, 68
pandemic. *See* Covid-19
Pareto principle, 119–20
participation, learning and, 61–62
peace, violence and, 27–28
Peddie, Norman, 40–41
people, operations compared to, 17–
    19
perfection, 32–33
    decisions and, 146–47
    progress compared to, 20
personal example, 150–57
personal leadership, 17–18
    Mandela and, 27–28
personal philosophy, 10–11, 13, 20,
    82–83
personal values, 17–18
perspectives, 188
    diverse, 145–46
philosophy, 192
    elders and, 83–84
    personal, 10–11, 13, 20, 82–83
Plato, 90, 92–93
policy, 140–41
    questions and, 71–72

205

Index

listening and, 99–100
promises and, 176
Sasson, Steve, 52
The School of Athens, 90, *92*, 92–93
science, 146
evolutionary, 12–13, 60, 106–8,
111–12, 139–40
of walking, 87
Seagram USA, 134–35
segregation, 22, 77–79
self-interest, 55, 187
Seneca, 166
services, of organizations, 56, 112–13,
123–24
Sexwale, Tokyo, 30
Shakespeare, William, *Julius Caesar*,
27
shareholders, value for, 67
siloed thought, 55–57
simplicity, 40, 112, 123, 186–87
stories and, 184–85
situation analysis, 108–9, 113
skills, 118, 183
questions as, 60
trust and, 174
social change, 32
social competence, 174
social contract, of organizations,
100–101
social norms, 77–79
Socrates, 60–61, 73
solutions, for problems, 50, 73, 74,
104, 138–39, 145, 174
upward feedback and, 101–2
South Africa, 25–29, 34, 76, 150–51,
185–86
apartheid in, 22–24, 30–31, 77–
79
challenges and, 32–33
learning and, 77–84
proverbs of, 83–84
Truth and Reconciliation Commission in, 30–31
stakeholders

interdependence of, 68–69
needs of, 18, 55–56, 140, 175
primacy of, 67
Starbucks, 69–70
static strategy, 104–7, 114, 195
status quo bias, 51–52
stories
disruption and, 189
emotion and, 185–86
influence and, 187–88
logic and, 130, 185
meaning and, 189
motivation and, 182–83
simplicity and, 184–85
strategic direction
focus on, 144
questions and, 67–68
Starbucks and, 69–70
strategic leadership, 18–19, 130
Mandela and, 31–34
Strategic Learning process, *109*, 111,
144
competition and, 112–13
Learn step of, 108–9, 112
as outside-in, 110
success and, 114–15
strategic logic, 130
strategic results, 51, 119–21
strategic thought, 90, 104–15
strategy
adaptation and, 106–11
change and, 104–6, 112
competitive advantage and, 104
costs and, 50
decisions and, 138
employees and, 182
interdependence and, 109–11
investors and, 68
military, 118
static, 104–7, 114, 195
time and, 89, 173
winning and, 111–12
strength, 27
of teams, 185–86

207

About the Author

W illie Pietersen was raised in South Africa and received a Rhodes Scholarship to Oxford University. After practicing law, he embarked on an international business career, serving as the CEO of multibillion-dollar businesses such as Lever Brothers Foods Division, Seagram USA, Tropicana, and Sterling Winthrop's Consumer Health Group.

In 1998 he was named Professor of the Practice of Management at the Columbia University Graduate School of Business. He specializes in strategy and the leadership of change and has served as an advisor to many global organizations in both the commercial and not-for-profit fields.

Pietersen's two prior books are *Reinventing Strategy* and *Strategic Learning*.

He has also written numerous articles and blogs on leadership and strategy, which can be viewed at www.williepietersen.com.

Printed in the USA
CPSIA information can be obtained
at www.ICGtesting.com
LVHW070014060924
790257LV00013B/21/J